# Maidstone Trams and Trolleybuses

Robert J Harley

Heathfield Publishing

  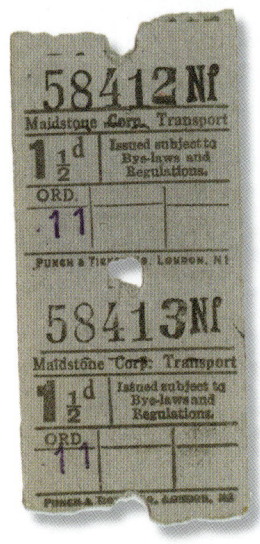 

Published by Heathfield Publishing in Heathfield, East Sussex, www.heathfieldpublishing.com © Robert J. Harley

# CONTENTS

1. **Kentish Trams**   6
2. **Trams of Kent**   13
3. **Orchards and Hop Gardens**   21
4. **War and Peace**   24
5. **Trackless**   33
6. **Consolidation**   41
7. **Trolleybus Triumphant**   47
8. **The Final Flourish**   56
9. **Abandonment and Beyond**   61

Maps   69

**Appendices:**
Livery   73
Rolling Stock - Tramcars   74
Rolling Stock - Trolleybuses   78
Preserved Vehicles   83
The Preservation of no.52   84
Advertisements   88
Fares   88
Overhead Equipment   90
Depots   91
The Southern Counties Touring
   Society   94
Bibliography   96

*Cover photo* The weather's fine – what better way for a transport enthusiast to spend a day than by photographing trolleybuses. Thankfully, John Bishop subscribed to this notion; his work stands as a valuable insight into a lost era. He has captured no.89 on film at the Fountain Inn, Barming. *John Bishop*

*Title page* Car 2 is depicted with its trolley retriever fixed to the rear dash. When they were delivered to Maidstone the trams sported no advertising; now the situation has changed completely. This vehicle is positively festooned with enticements for discerning shoppers. After a round of visits to the ironmongers, the drapers, the furniture store and the furriers, a soothing glass of Grant's Morello Cherry Brandy might be just the ticket.

*Opposite* We look back to the 1950s, when electric traction offered frequent, cheap and pollution free public transport in many British towns and cities. Here in Maidstone the trolleybus reflected local pride. *Peter Mitchell*

# Introduction and Acknowledgements

Many of my generation regard the 1950s as a 'golden age' of public transport in Great Britain. Steam locomotives dominated the railways; sleek expresses were complemented by slow trains which meandered along rural branch lines. The charm of this era was captured by poet, author and television personality, John Betjeman (1906-1984), and the rather whimsical nature of sleepy halts and forgotten country stations was given expression by the drawings of cartoonist, Rowland Emett (1906-1990).

Bus companies ran fleets of vehicles, both single and double deck, in a pleasing variety of liveries. It seemed that even the smallest hamlet could lay claim to a route linking it to the nearest county town. In urban areas municipal transport operators offering frequent services at reasonable fares were the focus of local pride. Residents rehoused in post war estates knew they were on the map, when the first corporation bus turned up outside their front gates.

There were mixed fortunes for the supporters of electric traction. The nation's remaining tramway systems were in terminal decline, but in many towns and cities the trolleybus appeared secure, for the time being at least. Against this background of plentiful, affordable public transport there was the seemingly inevitable growth of road traffic. The surge in car ownership throughout the decade was set to dictate town planning for the foreseeable future.

The buses and trolleybuses operating in Maidstone could fairly be said to embody all that was good in providing a decent public service attuned to local demands. The attractive livery of the fleet added to the appeal of the place. Although I lived in London, I was fortunate in visiting the town on many occasions. My journey would begin by boarding the Maidstone & District Motor Services coach at its stop in Eltham High Street. Following the main A20 trunk road into Kent, we would eventually cross the River Medway to arrive at the bus station in the town centre. Here one could observe the busy comings and goings of the dark green M&D vehicles. However, for me the real interest lay in the golden ochre and cream liveried trolleybuses operated by Maidstone Corporation. The system was compact, but there always seemed to be something happening; my curiosity was aroused by second hand vehicles, acquired from Hastings and Brighton, and by new route extensions into the Parkwood Estate. Sadly, this situation could not last and my interest waned in 1967, when electric traction ceased on the streets of the county town of Kent.

I am very grateful for the assistance of Bob Cook in compiling this book. Bob was born and brought up in Maidstone and was a witness at the fateful council meeting in 1964, which pronounced the death sentence on the trolleybuses.

John Bishop has been his usual genial self and was more than happy to contribute to the content of this book. He was out and about with his camera in Maidstone in its trolleybus heyday, and the results in both monochrome and colour can be enjoyed in the following pages. The street scenes are very evocative of a past era.

Special mention should be made of George Gundry and Stan Letts. Both had an affection for Maidstone in electric traction days, although in different eras. The author has fond memories of chatting to them at length about their experiences.

I owe much to Mick Webber, who has furnished many quality views and has generously given me access to his comprehensive archive of bus, trolleybus and tram material. I thank Dave Jones of the LCC Tramways Trust, who has lent photos from his collection. Hugh Taylor deserves a mention for giving permission to publish the work of photographer Peter Mitchell. Hugh has also contributed an interesting piece on the preservation Maidstone trolleybus no.52. Old school friend Richard Grover has kindly supplied colour views taken on our October 1966 visit. I thank Roger Smith for his excellent maps. Others worthy of an important mention are Peter Waller and Martin Jenkins; Lyndon Rowe, Bill Haynes, Colin Barker, Alan Jackson, Hugh Nicol, Richard Elliott, Geoffrey Baddeley, George Tapp and Ted Oakley. John Meredith supplied the information on the Southern Counties Touring Society and I am very grateful for his guidance and assistance.

I thank my own Maid of Kent – Janet, my wife – who was born and bred in Maidstone and claims never to have gone on a trolleybus! In her defence it should be stated that the suburbs where she lived were only served by corporation or M&D diesel buses. Her father, Ray Oxley, had very dim memories of riding on the open top deck of one of the town's trams. His mother, Milly Oxley, remembered travelling by tram in Gravesend and Chatham, where she resided before moving to Maidstone. As a former employee at Sharps, she used the trams on her way to work and valued their penny fares. At one stage of her life she caught the tram regularly between Hartnup Street and the town centre.

James Whiting of Capital Transport Publishing has given support, guidance and practical assistance with this book which has been much appreciated.

Finally, I am very grateful to all those people who have supplied pictures to complement the text. In spite of enquiries, it has been impossible to trace the original owners of some of the photos. My sincere apologies to anyone who sees their work unacknowledged.

As is well known, but bears repeating here, the village of Loose is pronounced 'looz' and Tovil has a short 'o' sound – certainly NOT toe-vil!

Robert J Harley
Heathfield, November 2016

# 1 Kentish Trams

The historic centre of Maidstone lies in the valley of the River Medway. Suburban development in the nineteenth century followed roads, many of which ascended from the river valley. An Edwardian guide book describes the town thus:

The County Town of Kent stands pleasantly situated on slopes above the Medway, here still navigable by barges. It has four main streets meeting near the Town Hall, with smaller branches and the usual fringe of suburban villas, while on the river banks are clustered mills and other signs of industry, paper and flour being dealt in here, as well as hops, the staple product of the district.

The River Medway bisects the town. This waterway plays a role in local usage and custom. Folk born on the western side of the river are referred to as 'Kentish Men' or 'Kentish Maids'; the eastern banks of the Medway mark the boundary of the territory of 'Men of Kent' or 'Maids of Kent'. Since the trams, and later the trolleybuses, crossed this divide, perhaps it should not seem too far fetched to apply the same human rules to them.

In fact it was from the west that the first tramway plans were mooted. In the 1870s there were voices raised along the Tonbridge Road towards the village of Barming in support of a horse tramway connection to the West Station on the South Eastern Railway (SER) and from there to the Cannon in the town centre. As regards these local landmarks, Maidstone West Station was opened on 25th September 1844 and the Russian gun was displayed in the 1850s as a souvenir of the Crimean War. Nothing came of the idea, until another scheme was proposed in 1881. Even then the hilly nature of the approaches to the town centre would have put serious constraints on equine powered tramways.

Apparently undeterred by this accident of geography the promoters of the 1881 proposals mapped out a comprehensive system with routes serving Tonbridge Road, London Road, Sandling Road, Ashford Road, Loose Road and Tovil Road. The intention was to provide a service for all parts of the borough. Unfortunately, those locals with influence, who were unimpressed by the plans, carried the day and the 1881 scheme foundered. It was said at the time that the horse and carriage folk saw no need for trams and that merchants and carters, who were responsible for transporting produce into the town, would find tramcars an obstruction in the highway.

There the matter rested until the last decade of the nineteenth century. In 1897 a transport revolution was taking place not many miles away in Dover. Contractors working for the progressive local authority had commenced construction of an electric tramway network. It is easy from a twenty-first century perspective to underestimate the impact of the new electric trams. They carried passengers cheaply and efficiently. They tackled hills and gradients. They enabled folk to live further from their place of work. They stimulated house building and ribbon development. At night they were a marvel of illumination. In an age mostly wedded to the candle, the oil lamp and the gas light, the brightly lit vehicles were acknowledged as a sign of the advancement of science.

Reports in the technical press stated that Stephen Sellon Assoc. M. Inst. C.E. had acted as a consultant to the project and was instrumental in persuading Dover Council to adopt the overhead wire system of current supply. Thus the name of this tramway expert came to the attention of the elected members in Maidstone. Several groups of local citizens made the trip to the Channel port and, impressed with what they saw, the belief grew that the County Town of Kent should join the electric revolution as soon as possible.

As a first necessary step, Maidstone Corporation decided in 1899 to put out tenders for the erection of a generating station. The completed building, situated at Fairmeadow next to the Medway, was opened on 19th December 1901, and was initially able to generate 675 kilowatts of electricity. This output capacity was further increased in 1907 and 1913. The way was now clear to add another important power station customer in the form of a municipal transport system and thus to expedite the introduction of electric traction to the town's streets.

In 1900 Stephen Sellon was appointed consultant to the corporation and he duly produced a report proposing a comprehensive tramway network for the town. At this time there were just over thirty-three thousand inhabitants living within the borough. After some debate Mr. Sellon must have been disappointed to hear that many of the routes he envisaged were deemed unachievable. However, a watered down version of his scheme was submitted to the Light Railway Commissioners in May 1902. It consisted of a line along Tonbridge Road to terminate at the borough boundary near the Fountain Inn, Barming. An extension of this track to a point 20 yards north west of the Bull Inn, Barming was also submitted to the Commissioners.

As the legal process progressed, the year of 1902 witnessed the opening of two other electric tramways in Kent, at Gravesend and at Chatham. A London syndicate submitted a Bill in the 1903 Parliamentary session for a proposed Rochester, Chatham, Gravesend & Maidstone Tramways Company. Of interest was the fact that the Bill stipulated either conventional tramways or 'motor cars worked by electricity on the overhead trolley system and not running on fixed rails'. This would have given the nation its first interurban trolleybus route. The vision of an interconnected network never came to pass, although the Chatham & District Light Railways Company did envisage extending its system to connect with neighbouring Maidstone, but again nothing concrete came of the proposal.

On 9th December 1903, the Barming route received the official green light. Contracts were awarded to Dick, Kerr & Co. Ltd, of Preston and the budget was set provisionally at £18,000. The official Board of Trade inspection of the new works took place on 12th July 1904.

In its autumn issue the *Electrical Review* published the following account:

As early as 1900 Mr. Stephen Sellon was called in by the Corporation to advise, and in due time the present scheme was finally determined upon; the Corporation, in its initial endeavour, has been prudent in not going to a large capital expenditure until it sees how the people of the district take advantage of the means of transit now afforded them.

The proposed scheme has been strongly opposed at every stage by certain sections of the ratepayers of Maidstone, and before the Light Railway Commissioners. Attempts were also made to defeat the application at the confirmation by the Board of Trade after the Light Railway Commissioners had signified their approval.

The line is, probably, an example of the economy which might well be followed both by companies and corporations contemplating the construction of tramways or light railways. The length of the line is about two miles, and the total cost, including the overhead equipment, six cars, car-shed, and all necessary appliances, cables, switchboards etc., will not, it is anticipated, exceed the sum of £20,000.

The system of track construction adopted is the ordinary grooved girder rail laid on a bed of concrete and paved as required with either wood, granite or local stone. The overhead work is span wire construction and on the under running system, the poles throughout the whole of the route being used for the purposes of street lighting. The power for the undertaking is supplied from the Corporation Electricity Works, which has undergone some few necessary alterations at the hands of Mr. Hoadley, the borough electrical engineer.

The whole of the work was executed by Messrs. Dick, Kerr & Co., and has been carried out in accordance with their usual high standard.

The track has been laid to a 3ft. 6in. gauge, with points in accordance with the latest practice, 13ft. long over all, of the extended leg type; the tongues which are 8ft. 6in. in length are specially machined in order to give cars easy entrance to the loops. The rails used are the British Standard No. 2 section, weighing 95 lbs. per yard; the joints are of the "Dicker" type. Tie bars are spaced at 6ft. intervals, and the track has been bonded throughout with 4/0 Neptune bonds.

The cars are of the double deck, single truck type, and are similar to those supplied to the Leicester Corporation, for Messrs. Dick, Kerr & Co., by the Electric Railway and Tramways Carriage Works, Ltd., Preston, who were the builders in this case also.

Each car has a seating capacity of 48 persons, 22 inside, and 26 outside. The electrical equipment consists of Dick, Kerr's standard D.B.1. form "C" type, arranged for rheostatic braking.

The car-shed has been constructed with a view to economical extension; the east wall, on which side the extension will probably be made, being panelled with 9in. brickwork between steel stanchions carrying the roof principals. The main shed proper contains pit accommodation for four cars, and provision has been made for offices, stores, paint, and repairing shops, etc.

We hear that excellent results have been obtained in the way of traffic receipts since the opening, on many occasions every car being required to carry the traffic over a route which has hitherto been devoid of any means of communication in the way of public conveyances, and although the tramway serves one of the least populated districts of Maidstone, it has carried a number of passengers equalling the whole population of that town 1½ times during the course of a week. It is, therefore, anticipated that a very satisfactory profit will be shown at the end of the first year's working.

We wish the Maidstone Corporation every success in its venture.

The great day arrived on 14th July 1904. Four decorated trams took part in the opening ceremony. The cortege was filled with the town's notables, as they made their way from the Queen's Monument in the centre of Maidstone to the depot at Barming and on to the end of the track opposite the Fountain Inn and a side street, which would later receive the appropriate name of Terminus Road.

The route was basically single track and loops. Double track existed from Broadway over the Medway Bridge to just short of the Cannon. Passing loops were situated at the Queen's Monument, Bower Place, Bowermount Road, Milton Street by the Admiral Gordon, Western Road and at Queen's Road by the Cherry Tree. In order to prevent collisions of tramcars travelling in opposite directions on single track, strict timetable working was enforced. There were no signals; several of the loops were in line of sight. This regulated control of tramcar movements to avoid collisions would also be instituted on subsequent extensions to the system, with the exception of the final approach to Loose terminus.

Powers for the extension of the permanent way to the Bull Inn, Barming were not granted. This caused some grumbling amongst the villagers beyond the borough boundary, who were denied the tram ride up the hill. The rest of the population took the trams to their hearts and ridership boomed. So much so that the original ten-minute service offered by the fleet of six tramcars was augmented in early 1905 by the addition of one extra vehicle.

Thus Maidstone Corporation became a tramway operator. It joined many other British municipalities in supplying quality public transport. The town had followed the Dover model of having a publicly owned system, rather than let private companies, as in Rochester, Chatham and Gravesend, run the show. However, pressure from ratepayers would always inject a note of caution to the proceedings. Other parts of the town would benefit from tram routes, but the amount the council could borrow to finance these extensions was subject to scrutiny. In the end, as we shall see, a number of consultative documents were commissioned for tracks to be laid to Sandling, Penenden Heath and on the London and Ashford roads, but nothing substantive was achieved.

The opening of the Maidstone tramways was an important event and, as such, attracted the attention of the local picture postcard publishers. It looks as if the mayor and the ceremonially dressed civic party have purloined the best vantage points on the leading tramcar. Those lower down the social pecking order have either been crammed on the following three trams or have had to make do by joining the watching throng of humanity.

The crowds have now departed. We view car 3 positioned at the end of the line by the Queen's Monument in the centre of town. This is a well known picture, which must have been sold in the hundreds. After all, Maidstonians were proud that they now possessed an up-to-date transport system, even if it only served one route to the western suburbs.

We remain by the Queen's Monument to witness the arrival of car 5 in the summer of 1904. This tram has yet to receive advertisements and is in 'as delivered' condition. Note the splendid array of headgear. In those days it was de rigueur to wear a hat. The style indicated not only the gender of the wearer, but also his or her social status. *Richard Rosa Collection*

Another familiar scene depicts car 3 on Tonbridge Road with St. Michael's Church nearby. In this hand coloured version a certain amount of licence by the artist has clothed the top deck passengers in a range of hues. At least whoever enhanced this picture has not 'painted' the tram green or blue!

Out on the Tonbridge Road car 2 is depicted in the very early days of the system. It has now acquired two advertisements on the dash either side of the fleet number and the circular catch for the trolley retriever apparatus. Note the smart uniforms of the motorman and conductor. It has been recorded that, since the tramway ran near the county asylum at Barming, staff and managers were frequent passengers. Surely, the gent in the bowler hat cannot be the famous Dr. Freud on a visit from Vienna? *Dave Jones Collection*

The tram in the distance is passing the entrance to the depot in Tonbridge Road. Car 3 waits at the passing loop opposite the Cherry Tree Inn. Queens Road leads off to the left of the picture. After negotiating the twists and turns of the journey from town, the road between here and the terminus was dead straight.

A smartly dressed lady cyclist holds a conversation with a representative of the local constabulary. Meanwhile the conductor on car 7 has time to assess the situation before the return journey to Barming. Between the dash advertisements for a laundry and a supplier of false teeth we can just make out the trolley rope attached to an American style circular trolley retriever. *Richard Stevenson Collection*

The conductor of car 3 looks towards the photographer as the tram makes its way through the hustle and bustle of the High Street. Note the early motor vehicle parked on the right of the picture.
*Richard Stevenson Collection*

# 2 Trams of Kent

Attention now switched to the urban area on the eastern bank of the Medway. In November 1904, application was made to the Light Railway Commission to grant powers under the title of *Maidstone Corporation Light Railways (Extensions)*. The following new routes were proposed:

*Railway No.1* Commencing in Boxley Road near the Bull Inn at Penenden Heath to terminate in Week Street near the Victoria Hotel.

*Railway No.2* Commencing in Boxley Road by a junction with Railway No.1 near the Royal George public house and terminating in Week Street near the Victoria Hotel.

*Railway No.3* Commencing in County Road by a junction with Railway No.2 at a point 16 yards, or thereabouts, south west of the junction of the said road with Well Road and terminating at the eastern end of Holland Street.

*Railway No.3A* Commencing in Well Road by a junction with Railway No.3 at a point 13 yards, or thereabouts, south east of the junction of the said road with County Road and terminating in the same road by a junction with Railway No.2 at a point 17 yards, or thereabouts, north west of the before mentioned junction of the said roads.

*Railway No.4* Commencing in Week Street by a junction with Railways Nos. 1 and 2 at their terminations above described and with Tramway No.3 authorized by the Chatham and District Light Railways Company Act 1903, at its commencement and terminating in High Street

*Railway No.4A* Commencing in Week Street by a junction with Railway No.4 at a point 18 yards, or thereabouts, north of King Street and terminating in Gabriel's Hill by a junction with Railway No.5 hereinafter described opposite the southern side of High Street.

*Railway No.5* Commencing in High Street by a junction with the existing Light Railway at its commencement and terminating in the Loose Road at or about the point which the boundary between the borough of Maidstone and the parish of Loose crosses the road.

*Railway No.6* Commencing in Loose Road by a junction with Railway No.5 at its termination above described and terminating near the working men's club at the top of Old Loose Hill.

At this point it is useful to know that many tramways were authorised under the Light Railways Act 1896. This measure was brought in to cut the red tape that surrounded the process of obtaining an Act of Parliament. The Light Railway Commissioners studied the plans, heard evidence from witnesses and then deliberated. They had the powers to reject or modify the proposals submitted to them. The Light Railways Act 1896 was repealed in its entirety by the Transport and Works Act 1992.

Unfortunately for Maidstone, the results of the November 1904 application were very disappointing and no progress was made in expanding the system.

The end of the line at Loose was used as a convenient jumping off point for many rambles in the picturesque Loose Valley. Prominent in this view are car 13, a cylindrical feeder pillar, a timetable and clock face to inform intending passengers of the next tram's arrival, and a rather rustic, but no less stylish, shelter for those waiting for their trip to town.

Objections were lodged in respect of the narrowness of certain streets. Week Street and Gabriel's Hill were two thoroughfares judged unsuitable for electric tramways. Of interest is Railway No.4 which would have linked the Chatham and Maidstone tramways. Passengers would be forever denied the experience of ascending Bluebell Hill by tramcar.

'If at first you don't succeed' must have been the motto of the personnel given the job of running the Maidstone Corporation Light Railways, because they tried again in 1906 and this time managed to obtain a positive result for the southern suburbs of the town. Wisely, Gabriel's Hill was left out of the scheme. Applications were made for lines to Loose and Tovil. The two new routes were to join the existing line at the Cannon by the junction of Mill Street and High Street. The two tramways would then diverge. The Tovil section was to run via College Road, King Edward Road and Tovil Road to a terminus at the foot of Tovil Hill by the paper mill. The light railway powers for connecting Loose with the rest of the system specified tracks being laid in Knightrider Street, Upper Stone Street and the length of Loose Road to a terminus by the Kings Arms near the summit of Old Loose Hill.

Construction commenced with priority being given to the Loose route. As the three way junction was being installed at the Cannon, the opportunity was taken in 1907 to double the track the whole length of High Street. Double track was also laid as far as Barton Road by the end of Upper Stone Street. In this latter thoroughfare there were short sections of a three track layout just after the turn out of Knightrider Street. It was thought that trams using this layout could avoid parked vehicles. At the beginning of Loose Road proper the line became single and was positioned on the eastern side of the carriageway out of the main traffic stream. No obstruction was caused by this example of gutter running, because there was plenty of space on the King's Highway for horse drawn vehicles; the motor age had yet to arrive in force.

Back in the early years of the twentieth century there was precious little other traffic on the roads. Car 10 could stand in the highway with no risk of causing an obstruction at Loose terminus. Driver and conductor pose proudly for the photographer. Of note is the small instruction above the motorman's head. It reads SWING THE POLE THIS SIDE (plus the appropriate arrow).

Although there was some ribbon development, parts of Loose Road still resembled a country lane. At the junction with Pickering Street there was a two road depot or stabling shed. Just before this location the single tram track crossed over to the western side of the carriageway and remained thus until the terminus by the Kings Arms, Loose. Passenger operation over this section commenced on 16th October 1907. The section from the Loose terminus to the first passing place, which bore the name of Dr. Jones' Loop, was worked initially on a token system. This ensured that no two trams could meet on the blind bend at the top of the hill near the borough boundary.

The new route to Tovil possessed one passing loop in King Edward Road and the line was then single until Tovil Hill was reached with its length of double track. The opening ceremony took place on 9th January 1908. The network was now complete and those tramless suburbs to the north of the town centre would now have some years to wait for a reliable public transport in the shape of the motor bus.

An increase in the size of the fleet was now required to provide for passengers on the Loose and Tovil extensions. Eight new trams were delivered in July 1907, followed by another two vehicles in the December. Since these trams were fitted with conventional British swivel head trolleys, the running wires did not need to be placed centrally over the track, as was the case on the Barming route where, initially, trams had sported American style fixed head trolleys and trolley retrievers. The original members of the fleet, cars 1-7, were converted to swivel head trolleys and their trolley retrievers were removed to be replaced by a trolley rope. Headlights fixed on the canopy over the motorman were moved to the conventional position on the dashes.

Tovil once had a branch railway, a tram route and the fabled Tovil Treacle Mines. Car 12 is pictured at the bottom of the hill, one of the steepest gradients on the system, just a few yards away from the end of the track. The trolley pole has been positioned for the return journey to the High Street.

Funds were available in 1908 to purchase a works vehicle in the shape of a water car for use in summer to keep the dust down. When the weather turned wintry, this vehicle could employ its two revolving snow brooms to clear a path for service trams. Unfortunately, being assigned to the water car was treated as some sort of penance by the crews. It was blessed with the nickname 'Dreadnought' and was considered a very unwieldy beast to operate.

The water car was a substantial looking vehicle. Allegedly it was difficult to drive and therefore unpopular with staff. Here it lays over at the Barming terminus outside the Fountain Inn. Style & Winch was a local brewer, based at St. Peter's Street in the town. Brewing ceased in 1965 and the premises was later demolished. In recent years after a period of closure the Fountain Inn has taken on a new role as an Indian restaurant and conference facility. *Dave Jones Collection*

At the top end of the High Street the tram terminus is occupied by car 11 and the water car. From the look of the roadway the latter vehicle must have just performed its duties in dampening down the dust and clearing some of the detritus. With equine power still in vogue any rose grower with a shovel would have had a field day! As the century progressed with an increase in motor traffic and better road surfaces the need for the water car diminished.

From 1910 the Tovil route was cut back from Queen's Monument to terminate here by the triangular junction at the Cannon. As soon as the driver boards his charge, car 8 will proceed towards the photographer and along Mill Street.

At first, all three routes started from the Queen's Monument; however, this arrangement proved impractical and from 1910 only the Barming service terminated here. Cars for Tovil and Loose then departed from the Cannon. A slight variation occurred in the summer of 1908, when Loose bound cars terminated at the West Station. On the indicator blind this location was described as S.E. STATION. Passenger levels on the Barming and Loose routes remained fairly healthy, but it was soon apparent that the Tovil line was somewhat of a white elephant. The management decided to cut costs by purchasing a one man operated demi car single decker to maintain a shuttle service between the foot of Tovil Hill and the Cannon. The idea was to save on manpower costs and also to trim the electric bill.

In 1910 yet another report was commissioned in respect of an extension of the tramways to join with the neighbouring system at Chatham. Had this plan reached fruition, it is interesting to speculate whether a branch along Boxley Road to Penenden Heath would have been included as a later addition. Voices were also raised in support of a new service along Sutton Road in the direction of Sutton Valence. This line would have traversed a very rural area. Unsurprisingly, although these projects may have looked good on paper, they failed to cut any ice with those councillors who controlled the corporation's purse strings. It has been said that the disappointing results from the Tovil route effectively put a large spanner in the works of the tramway expansionists.

The one man operated single decker trundled back and forth to Tovil. At peak periods it offered a service on the line and it could also be seen operating to Loose at other times during the day. Therefore, it must be assumed that this transfer left the Tovil route devoid of rolling stock and the few intending passengers had to walk at least as far as College Road to get the tram.

Out on the Tonbridge Road an official photograph is recorded of demi car 18. Passengers boarded and alighted from the front end of this vehicle.

As can be seen, the tram tracks occupied the left side of the broad High Street, before the road narrowed just past the Cannon. The tram going to Loose dates the view to the summer of 1908, when this service terminated at Maidstone West Station. A sign of the impending future is the MAIDSTONE MOTOR GARAGE. Although, from looking at this picture, the proprietors would be hard put to find any customers.

At the other end of the line from the town centre car 9 waits to return to S.E. STATION (Maidstone West). It was said that this short lived terminal was at the behest of Councillor Vaughan, who had business interests nearby. The announcement on the back of the tram is a tribute to the power of positive advertising in the triumph of hope over experience. We are informed that 'it doesn't hurt a bit' when teeth are extracted by FORD'S HUMANE SYSTEM. Luckily for the dentist at 50 King Street there was no Advertising Standards Agency in 1908 to check the veracity of the claim!

In 1879 Maidstone Bridge was rebuilt under the supervision of Sir Joseph Bazalgette, the eminent Victorian civil engineer, who was also responsible for the Victoria Embankment in London. Work began in 1926 on widening Bazalgette's structure across the Medway. This view is taken from the west bank of the river. Although no trams have entered this scene, we can note the neat arrangement of the overhead wires and the sweep of the double tracks as they cross the bridge to enter the High Street.

# 3 Orchards and Hop Gardens

Although Maidstone was not known as an important tourist centre and still less as a holiday destination, the town did possess a hinterland of attractive countryside. The electric trams terminated within walking distance of open fields, woodland, orchards and hop gardens. For an outlay of a couple of pennies a town dweller could leave factory life and crowded streets behind. Books and leaflets were published to describe walks of interest to ramblers.

It is worth quoting from *A Guide to the Borough of Maidstone* by A.S. Lamprey, published in 1914:

Visitors to the town are earnestly recommended to tour the Barming and Loose routes, when they find that, as they approach these termini, they are lifted to a fairly high altitude into a bracing atmosphere and are in the midst of lovely scenery. The River Medway, which affords good sport for anglers, may be reached within a few minutes walk of the Barming Terminus, and those who admire woodland scenery will find one of the loveliest and most extensive woods in the County of Kent but a little way off. Within two minutes' walk there is also a recreation ground on Barming Heath, which is open to the public.

On the Loose route, at the end of the penny stage, the passenger will pass close by the Maidstone Cemetery. A little further on the route to the right is the Maidstone Church Institute Playing Field.

Owing to the bracing air of the Loose district and a frequent service of tram cars, building operations have gone on most extensively during the last few years, so that it has now become one of the suburbs of the town.

Arriving at the terminus, visitors are urged to walk down the hill into the picturesque village of Loose, and thence on through the valley to the hamlet of Tovil where the cars may be rejoined.

Special return fares are issued to Loose during the summer months (May to September) on Wednesdays and Saturdays after 1pm at 3d each, children half price, available for returning by the same or Tovil route.

A Zoological Collection and Tea Garden has recently been opened at Tovil Court, situated near the tram terminus on the Tovil route. Single fare 1d, children under 12 half price, return fare for adults 1½d.

After leaving the terminus by the Cannon trams proceeded along Mill Street and crossed over the River Len. A few yards further on was the Tithe Barn. Built in the 14th Century and now a listed Grade One monument, the Tithe Barn was once used as a stables for the nearby Archbishop's Palace. The double track here extended all the way to Barton Road at the start of Loose Road. All Saints is the parish church of Maidstone. Completed in the late 1390s, the building on the east bank of the Medway has rightly been described as the finest example of Perpendicular Style in the United Kingdom. It was a well known sight for top deck tram passengers. In the foreground is the junction of the Tovil and Loose routes at the corner of Mill Street and Knightrider Street.

Season tickets at cheap rates are issued on all routes, quarterly, half-yearly, and yearly. Further particulars may be obtained from the Tramways Office, Barming.

A further note was added on the Maidstone Zoo at Tovil Court. One would presume this attraction was music to the ears of the corporation tramways, because its presence would boost takings on the Tovil line.

Surrounding the Zoological Gardens are 15½ acres of gardens, well timbered paddocks, and a lake encompassed by wooded walks. Though the Gardens are situated in the Borough of Maidstone, with trams passing the Entrance Lodge, a visitor to them might well imagine himself in the depths of the country, so secluded and rural are the surroundings.

Visitors leaving the train at Maidstone East Station had to walk along Week Street to reach the trams. There is some evidence to suggest that this view was taken in that fateful summer of 1914. The time according to the Town Hall clock is coming up to 1pm. A tram waits to convey passengers along the Tonbridge Road to Barming.

The photographer has now set up a tripod on the opposite side of the Queen's Monument. We have a front view of the Leyland lorry, whose tailgate featured in the last scene. Waiting next to the lorry are a couple of individuals, who may be employed by Maidstone Corporation Tramways. Unfortunately we still do not know the fleet number of the tram to Barming. Note the horse drawn open carriages plying for hire on this summer's day over a century ago.

St. Michael's Church tower and an elegant traction standard feature prominently in this view of Tonbridge Road. The tram route was laid out as single track and loops. In the distance by Bowermount Road two trams occupy a passing place. There were no signals. Drivers relied on line of sight to avoid meeting a tram going in the opposite direction on the single line.

After the First World War the trams continued to serve as a means for people on their days off to explore the rural landscape. The most popular country walks began at the two termini of Barming and Loose. Towards the end of the tramway era the bucolic charms of the Loose Valley were being extolled in books such as *The Enchanted Road* by Donald Maxwell, which was published in 1927. Although the journey from town had by then lost some its countrified flavour; house building had followed the tram tracks almost as far as the borough boundary. A couple of fine specimens of oast houses still stood at the corner of Plains Avenue. These served to remind passengers of one of the principal crops grown in the area. Kentish hops were used by several local breweries such as Fremlins and Style & Winch.

A favourite excursion was to leave the tram at Shernold Pond by the Swan Inn. Adjacent to this hostelry were tea gardens and these were advertised as 'The Swan Inn Pleasure Gardens for Families and Parties – Trams Stop At Door'. If the attractions of the Swan could be postponed till later, then walkers were advised to follow Cripple Street to the Mill Pond at Bockingford. The Bockingford Arms, which had been the subject of a popular postcard view by the artist A.R. Quintin (1853-1934), also possessed a tea garden. After quenching their thirst, ramblers would head south following the river past orchards, until the picturesque village of Loose was reached. Finally, there was a climb up the hill to the Kings Arms, where the familiar light brown and cream tramcar would be waiting. At the other end of the line walks led from the terminus at Fountain Inn along Farleigh Lane to the Medway. The river could also be reached via East Barming and Barming Bridge. There were extensive fruit orchards in this area.

# 4 War and Peace

The most noticeable initial effect of the declaration of war on 4th August 1914, was the rush by many male Maidstonians to join the colours. As was to be expected, the Maidstone Corporation Light Railways also sacrificed personnel to the military. Of necessity female staff were recruited. They took the place of tram conductors and six women were trained as drivers. Throughout the town factories were put on a war footing. Engineering works including the famous Tilling-Stevens concern found themselves, as one contemporary observer ironically stated, 'in the business of turning plough shares into swords'. Even the premises of Messrs Sharp, where they manufactured large quantities of 'Kreemy Toffee', experienced an upsurge of demand to satisfy the sweet tooth of the British Expeditionary Force on the Western Front.

The town's working population needed public transport and the trams coped as best they could. Aside from travelling by train, there were few alternatives to Shanks' pony. Private motoring was restricted to the affluent and such bus services as existed, were subject to delays, mechanical breakdowns and overcrowding. In the circumstances the twelve tramcars, required to satisfy passenger demand, performed beyond expectations. However, service was still spasmodic on the Tovil route and later in the war the decision was taken to conserve electricity. Trams ceased to run on this section except for two workings at shift times in the Paper Mill. The Sunday timetable on the Loose route was also curtailed and cars ran after two o'clock in the afternoon. Maintenance arrears took their toll and in response to other factors, such as shortages of personnel and uncertain electricity supplies, there was a cut in the available numbers of rolling stock. In 1918 the timetable was worked by only nine vehicles.

Car 9 is depicted in wartime. The tram crew and some of the local kids have been captured on film. As in many other towns in the kingdom female staff were recruited to help keep the service running. Note the conductress's bell punch, whistle and ticket rack in her leather cash satchel.

Car 11 is depicted on the terminal siding at the entrance to Mill Street. A couple of passengers take their seats on the top deck, while the driver stows his timecard by the front bulkhead window. On the left of the picture an inspector gives an eye to the conductor who is swinging the trolley pole. It is probably Maidstone Cricket Week, hence the flags draped from the buildings and traction standards. Kent County Cricket Club used to play at Mote Park. The ground was opened in 1857. *Hugh Nicoll/ National Tramway Museum*

On a normal workday before six o'clock in the morning three trams entered service from Tonbridge Road Depot. At the other end of the line Loose Shed supplied one tram. Two hours later to cater for passengers on their way to work a further two tramcars, one from each depot, were pressed into service. At one stage during the hours of daylight one of the Loose Shed cars was swapped for a Tonbridge Road vehicle, so that essential maintenance could be carried out. Around midday the service was augmented by two more trams from the main depot. After the evening peak vehicles gradually returned to their home bases; at least one tram was always stationed at Loose Shed. The last Tovil car ran at eight o'clock in the evening. Although this was the Cinderella route, its fortunes took a turn for the better in 1919, when double deckers returned to cater for the workers at the paper mill. This pattern of operation throughout the town was maintained during the tramway era.

After the end of the war in November 1918 the female platform staff were gradually replaced by their male colleagues. Essential track work maintenance was carried out on the Barming route. It was reported that some of the paving adjacent to the tram rails on the Tonbridge Road had lifted and needed to be repaired. The blame was placed on several mechanised columns, which the military had used to transport equipment, men and munitions across the county. They obviously churned up the highway. It was significant that motorised transport based on the internal combustion engine came of age during the conflict on the Western Front. In the immediate post war years lorry and bus technology would advance at a pace.

We now enter one of the most interesting periods in the history of public transport in Maidstone. The decade of the 1920s would see important changes. First on the agenda was the provision of services to the northern part of the town. By 1922 there was no further talk of extending the tramways. A viable alternative to railbound vehicles was being offered by motor buses. Yet another avenue for the transport committee to explore lay with a promising new fixed route technology in the trackless tram or trolleybus. In November 1922 twelve double deck, covered top trolleybuses replaced trams on the Nechells route in Birmingham. The vehicles were supplied by the Railless Electric Traction Company (RET) and had bodywork by Charles H. Roe of Leeds.

Positive reports in the technical press plus the lobbying of the RET resulted in a stream of transport professionals eager to inspect the new system. In early 1923 the chairman of Maidstone Corporation Light Railways and the manager of the undertaking, A.T. Lambert, made the journey to the West Midlands as guests of the RET. As with many of their contemporaries they were impressed by the Birmingham set up and, no doubt, they returned to Kent with some useful ideas. However, it must not be assumed that they were in a hurry to dispense with the trams. It is far more likely that they envisaged the new trolleybuses as the solution to the vexed question of supplying quality public transport in areas not served by the trams.

At the turn of the century the open top tramcar fairly represented the state of the art as regards electric traction; however, two decades later this was no longer the case. Many British tramway operators in cities and even some quite modest affairs in smaller towns were investing in covered top rolling stock. The thinking behind this move was that inside the upper saloon of the tramcar would be a more hospitable place in inclement weather. The Maidstone management could have taken a leaf out of the book of their county colleagues in Gravesend and Dover, where top deck passengers were finally getting a roof over their heads. In the event nothing was done to modernise the tram fleet.

We view the High Street towards the end of the tramway era. As originally laid the tramline at this location was single, but with the opening of new routes to Tovil and Loose double track was substituted.

If there is one picture that typifies the last years of the Maidstone trams, then this view at the Wheatsheaf on Loose Road fits the bill. On a glorious spring day in the late 1920s car 17 waits at a passing loop for its opposite number to arrive from town. The conical roofs of the oast houses on Plains Avenue can be seen on the extreme left of the picture. They give a clue to the nature of this location before ribbon development of housing in the first three decades of the twentieth century.

The Maidstone Corporation Act 1923 gave the local authority powers to operate trolleybuses. The Act specified one main route from High Street to Penenden Heath via Week Street, Sandling Road, Hope Street, Randall Street, Lowe Boxley Road and Boxley Road. A very short branch was authorised along Albert Street. Looking at this Act it would appear that the trolleybus was in a favoured position. Further evidence presented itself when local firm, Tilling-Stevens, was given permission by the council to test out trolleybus chassis by placing one trolley pole on the tramway overhead. The operator would then connect a metal skate to the test vehicle, in order to trail it along the tram rails to complete the electrical circuit. It is probable that the initial batch of trolleybuses for Wolverhampton were put through their paces in this fashion.

Tilling-Stevens did receive a local order. Contrary to expectations, on 7th April 1924, motor buses were employed on a service from Penenden Heath to London Road. Three petrol-electric, single deck buses appeared in corporation colours. Some weeks before the launch of the first motor bus route, it was decided by the Light Railways Committee at a meeting on 27th February 1924, that when the Barming route infrastructure – track and overhead – came up for renewal, serious consideration would be given to replacing trams with trolleybuses. Members of the committee then spent the next few months deliberating on the future direction of the undertaking. During the following two years the fate of the town's tramcars was well and truly sealed.

In January 1926 the undertaking was renamed from Maidstone Corporation Light Railways to Maidstone Corporation Transport. Committee members could look back on a decade of improving finances. The tramways account had been in deficit until 1914, when the debt outstanding had shrunk to £821. Working costs had been kept to a minimum, so that by 1928 the transport department was in credit to the tune of £30,000. Thus, it was from this sound basis that plans could be made for the future.

The events of the mid 1920s were described by A.T. Lambert in an article for *The Tramway and Railway World* magazine, dated 12th July 1928:

The Barming route, on which a new system of trolley vehicles has just been inaugurated, has always been the principal route of the undertaking and shows a profit. Commencing at the borough boundary adjacent to the village of Barming, it runs along the main Tonbridge Road until it is intersected by the London Road (the main road between London and Folkestone), coming into the High Street, where heavy and congested traffic is met with.

In 1923 the writer of this article reported to the Maidstone Town Council that the undertaking, so far as the Barming route was concerned, could not last longer than to March 1928. It was, therefore, necessary to investigate and report on the cost of various types of transport. It was soon evident that the proposal to relay the tramway track and provide new rolling stock was quite beyond consideration, as this would involve a further capital outlay of some £65,000.

In 1924 the corporation deputed the chairman, Councillor T. Armstrong, the vice chairman, Councillor G. Larking, and the manager to visit other towns where trolley omnibuses, petrol omnibuses, or other suitable means of transport were in operation, and to report the results of their inspections and make recommendations. Councillor F. Conner, now Mayor of Maidstone, always a keen and enthusiastic supporter of trolley omnibuses, accompanied the party on the tour. In the autumn of 1926 application was made to Parliament for a Provisional Order under the Maidstone Corporation (1923) Act, to convert all existing tramway routes and to add a new route 1½ miles long. This order was granted in the spring of 1927.

The location is the western bank of the Medway with the road bridge in the background. The date is 27th December 1927. Trolleybus wires have been installed in preparation for driver training. The only public transport available during this inundation consists of two horse drawn carts, which were ferrying passengers to higher ground.

This account was penned after the inauguration of the trolleybus route to Barming; however, before this could happen, there was plenty of work to complete. Steel traction standards in use since the opening of the tramways had to be reinforced with concrete and new standards had to be erected to cope with the extra wiring needed for trolleybuses. The trolley wires themselves were 4/0 SWG grooved hard drawn cadmium copper; they were spaced at 15 inches apart. Turning circles were erected at Fountain Inn, Barming and at the Queen's Monument, High Street. The one fly in the ointment was the state of the roadway with existing tram tracks, because access to Barming Depot had to be maintained for these vehicles. The sections of track from the depot to the Fountain and from Mill Street junction to the Queen's Monument were scheduled to be lifted.

Trolleybus wires had certainly been erected by December 1927 in the town centre and along Tonbridge Road. They are in evidence in postcard views of the great flood of 27th December, when the River Medway burst its banks. Such inundations were not unknown in the area. A previous incident affecting the tramways had occurred in October 1909. The corporation supplied various carts and converted charabancs drawn by horses to convey tram passengers to the nearest dry ground. Although getting ahead of our story, flooding was looked on as a sort of occupational hazard by the transport department and watery 'events' in 1953 and 1955 also disrupted trolleybus services.

The final section of this chapter is based on an account of two visits by George Gundry to Maidstone in the 1920s. In several interviews with your author in the early 1990s, George was in sparkling form as he recounted events of almost seven decades earlier. The following adds material from letters to the author:

Right from an early age I was interested in tramways. My first memories are of the splendid London United tramcars that linked Wimbledon with Kingston-upon-Thames and Hampton Court. We had regular summer holidays away from London. We visited Southend-on-Sea, the Isle of Thanet, Hastings, Bexhill and Eastbourne. All places except Eastbourne had tramway networks to keep a child like me very entertained. My parents, I have to say, used to indulge my passions and they must have spent many pennies on tram rides round the boulevards of Thorpe Bay, doing the whole journey from Westgate to Ramsgate and, of course, going round the circular route in Hastings and then out to Cooden Beach on the tram.

Walks and rambles in the countryside – and there was a lot of that around the fringes of London, before the suburban housing boom of the 1930s – were not as interesting for me, but in those days kids were more obedient to their parents and I accepted the climb up Leith Hill or looking at the carpets of bluebells in the woods as a part of my education, if you like. One day in the summer of 1922, I was told we were going for a country walk in the Garden of England. This involved a train journey to Maidstone. Just before we got to our destination my folks mentioned that we were going to see trams in Maidstone.

You can imagine my disappointment after we disembarked at Maidstone East Station and there were no trams or even a sign of overhead wires or tramlines. I must have looked crestfallen. My father asked for directions from a porter at the station. When Dad said the word "Loose", the chap corrected his pronunciation. My father was intrigued. He always fancied himself as a bit of a linguist and loved rather eccentric sounding English place names of which there were a lot in Kent at that time. I took my camera with me. It wasn't that good a camera, but then who in the early 1920s was taking photos of trams? At least the photos have given me some memories of my journeys by tram.

One of this country's premier tram enthusiasts was George Gundry. This snap of his is included for its historic value. It is of Loose terminus in the summer of 1922. Although taken on a 'basic' camera, we can still make out the conductor who is about to swing the trolley pole. Passengers on the lower deck are afforded some protection from the rays of the sun by drawing the curtains. *George Gundry*

Car 2 has just deposited the Gundry family outside the Fountain Inn, Barming. Young George was given the task of recording the scene for posterity. *George Gundry*

The weather was warm and we walked towards the town centre. Suddenly the road opened out to what looked like a market place. There standing in the roadway was the object of my desire. A brown and cream painted open top tramcar, with the word BARMING on the indicator blind, appeared about to depart. Just before the car left, in response to our question, the conductor told us to walk a couple of hundred yards down the High Street to catch the Loose tram at the Cannon. My parents' remark: "I hope it's not loaded!" failed to produce a smile from the conductor, who then went about his business.

As I remember it, the tram to Loose was parked next to the pavement on a sort of siding off the main double track. It was a fine day, so we went to sit on the top deck. Soon we were on our way and the conductor came up the stairs to take our fares. Maidstone trams came in two varieties – short and long. We were on one of the short ones. I believe the lower saloon with its bench seats was three or four feet shorter than the original batch of trams. Those ones, the long variety, appeared to keep to the Barming route. On our tram with its restricted seating on the top deck, there were only a few spare seats, as we made our way through narrow streets. At the foot of a hill leading out of the town we paused at an ALL CARS STOP HERE sign. It was also a chance for the inbound car from Loose to pass us.

There were some interesting old houses and several seemed to lean out over the pavement in the direction of the tram. As I remember, a horse drawn farm cart was plodding up the hill and the carter, on noticing our approach, shifted his charge to the other side of the road. We continued our slow and steady climb up the hill.

When we reached the top, the road opened out, but the tram track continued to hug the left hand kerb. Luckily in those days there were no parked vehicles to block our way. The housing along this part of the journey was solidly middle class villas, as they used to call them. As we proceeded further from the town, the number of houses diminished. From the top deck I caught glimpses of open fields and fruit orchards.

Although trams were only meant to stop where there was a car stop sign, the driver of our vehicle obviously knew his regulars and before we got to Loose he had slowed down several times, so that people could get off before a recognised stop. I remember one chap in a tweed jacket, who alighted from the tram right outside the front gate of his cottage. In my eyes he was very lucky living in a country cottage next door to a tram route.

The next building that caught my eye was a small tram depot built in a field next to the road. A single track led off our line and then split into two tracks within the car shed. As we passed, a quick peer inside told me that the place was empty. There seemed to be nobody about. The overhead wires leading to the depot were slack and drooped a bit. No doubt the conductor had to hold the trolley rope when cars entered the depot, otherwise there would be a dewirement. And then from the small depot to the terminus the tram went down a slope until the end of the line. As I recall, there was a high stone wall one side of the road. There was double track at the terminus. For us the points were set straight ahead and we slowed to a halt.

Our ride was over, but we waited to watch the conductor turn the trolley pole for the return journey. I believe on Maidstone trams you could only swing the pole in one direction. I took a photo of the tram with the conductor about to untie the trolley rope. After observing this scene, we went down the hill and started our country walk proper.

Not long before the trolleybuses replaced trams in Maidstone I made another trip to the town. On my last visit I had managed to ride the route to Barming, but had not had a chance to visit the main depot on Tonbridge Road. I put that right on this occasion. I boarded the tram, one of the long ones, at the Queens Monument. By this time there was more motor traffic about and generally less horse drawn vehicles. There were several lorries parked near the tram terminus and before we could start, a brewer's dray had to clear the tracks further down the High Street.

Although I had only a passing interest in buses, I noted a couple of single deckers in corporation colours. I rather hoped their appearance did not augur badly for the trams. In the event, as we know, only the Tovil line was replaced by motor buses. I believe they were manufactured by local firm Tilling-Stevens. Were they petrol-electric like the trams along Hastings front? If they were, they made a different noise to the seaside trams at Hastings. The buses were probably better maintained. They made a sort of low growling sound.

By the Cannon at the junction with Mill Street a car for Loose was waiting. The conductor had already turned the trolley and several passengers were getting on. We negotiated the triangular junction and then the motorman applied power to begin the approach to the Medway bridge. The bridge itself had been widened since my last visit and the relaid tram tracks looked in good condition. Unfortunately, the same couldn't be said for some of the rails in Tonbridge Road. A well known spot for picture postcard firms was the view of St Michael's Church. It was near here that the tram driver slowed right down. There was what is known as a dropped joint in the track. It was single track and loops all the way to Barming. As we passed over the sunken rails the tram bucked and swayed a bit, and then we stopped. I fancy the driver must have thought the lifeguard tray had dropped. After making a quick check we were on our way again. I'm fairly certain, had the lifeguard tray dropped, we would all have heard it bumping over the woodblock setts in the road.

There were rows of houses on either side of the route. This was typical tramway territory, of the sort that you could find all over the country, where trams on single track would wait at loops for their opposite number coming in the other direction. Although I had intended to go all the way to the end of the line, I broke my journey outside the depot. I knocked on the door of what looked like an office. Before anybody answered a fitter appeared round the corner. I asked for permission to look round and he offered to show me what was going on.

Car 6 had been jacked up and the truck run out from underneath the car body. I recognised immediately the standard Brill 21E model as used in Britain and indeed all over the world. As a four wheel truck it was solid and reliable. Another chap in overalls was checking one of the axle boxes. My fitter guide pointed out various features of the truck. He agreed with me they were a good piece of engineering. The only problems came in the early years of the system when the staff had to deal with a number of broken axles. The simple solution was to attach wheels to thicker axles! He said the manufacturers had compensated the corporation for all the work involved in sorting out the problem.

I said good-bye to my guide and walked the few hundred yards to the tram terminus opposite the Fountain Inn. The single line branched into two sidings. When the next tram arrived, I took my seat on the top deck for the ride back to town.

My abiding memories of Maidstone trams were that they were well maintained and looked splendid in their unusual livery. As I have said, there were some problems with parts of the permanent way, but this should not detract from the general positive impression.

Professor Hugh Nicol was a scientist, broadcaster and author, who also took a great interest in tramways. Here he has ridden to the end of the line on car 11. At Tovil the motorman and conductor pose for his camera. *Hugh Nicol/National Tramway Museum*

# 5 Trackless

The end for the Barming trams came on 30th April 1928 and the new trolleybus service commenced the next day. A ceremonial procession full of invited guests left the High Street outside the Town Hall. Heading the line was no.18, driven by A. Wood, which departed at 11 am. Unfortunately, this inaugural start was not staggered and an abrupt halt interrupted the event, as the overloaded fuses blew in the nearby section box.

As far as we know, the last tramcar in passenger service from the Fountain to town passed completely unnoticed; there was no valedictory celebration. Before the cessation of the tramway, Tonbridge Road had been the scene of driver training on the newly delivered eight trolleybuses. So as not to interfere with the trams, the familiarisation of drivers with their vehicles and route took place at night.

Sadly, finance was not available for a new operating home for the trolleybuses. They were housed in the old tram depot on Tonbridge Road, where space was at a premium. Whereas the railbound vehicles, being double ended, could move in and out with the minimum of fuss, this was not the case with the trolleybuses. Each vehicle, on taking up service, had to reverse out of the depot gates into the main road. Inevitably as motor traffic increased, this manoeuvre became risky. Staff had to be alert and conductors would station themselves on the highway ahead of their charges to make sure everything went off safely.

The Queen's Monument to Barming trolleybus service is now in operation. Tracks and overhead wires have been retained so that the remaining trams on the Tovil and Loose routes can gain access to the depot. Trolleybus no.11 heads out of town, as a sister vehicle unloads opposite the Cannon. A Corporation single deck motor bus is seen in the High Street. Trams, trolleybuses, buses and steam trains serving the local stations – what more could a transport enthusiast want!

# J. W. COURTENAY Ltd.

## Tramway and Omnibus Advertising Contractors

Established Half-a-Century.

## SOLE CONTRACTORS FOR

Liverpool Corporation Tramways.
Birmingham Corporation Tramways and Omnibuses.
Portsdown & Horndean Light Railway Co.
Wakefield & District Light Railway.
Calcutta Tramways Co., Ltd.
Mandalay Electric Tramways.
Newcastle-on-Tyne Corporation Tramways and 'Buses.
Burton-on-Trent Corporation Transport Department.
Scarborough Electric Tramways Co., Ltd.
Cawnpore Electric Tramways.
Hastings & District Electric Tramways Co., Ltd.
Gosport and Fareham Tramways Co.
Doncaster Corporation Tramways.
Delhi Electric Tramways.
Gloucester Corporation Light Railways.
Ilford Corporation Tramways.
Halifax Corporation Tramways.
Huddersfield and District Omnibuses.
Malta Tramways Company.

Exeter Corporation Tramways.
Rotherham Corporation Tramways and Omnibuses.
Dundee, Broughty Ferry & District Tramways.
Barrow-in-Furness Corporation Tramways.
Maidstone Corporation Tramways and Omnibuses.
Yorkshire (West Riding) Electric Tramways Co., Ltd.
Croydon Corporation Tramways.
Stockton and Thornaby Corporation Joint Tramways.
Stockton Corporation Omnibuses.
St. Helens Corporation Tramways.
Ipswich Corporation Trolley Omnibuses.
Derby Corporation Tramways.
Portsmouth & Hambledon Omnibuses.
Llandudno and Colwyn Bay Electric Railway, Ltd.
Wigan Corporation Tramways.
West Riding Automobile Co., Ltd.
Newport Corporation Tramways and Omnibuses.
Dearne District Light Railways.
Leeds and Wakefield Omnibuses.
Southampton Corporation Omnibuses.

## HIGHEST RATES PAID FOR SOLE RIGHTS
### ON ANY SYSTEM OF TRAMWAYS OR OMNIBUSES

AMBERLEY HOUSE, NORFOLK STREET, LONDON, W.C.2.

This trolleybus line up of the Maidstone fleet was staged as part of an advertising campaign.

A member of the Maidstone constabulary shows an interest in trolleybus no.12 as it takes on passengers at the town terminus. As can be seen here, the new trolleybuses looped round the Queen's Monument at the top of the High Street. This card is postmarked November 1930.

The tram shed by Pickering Street on the Loose Road now assumed a greater importance, as it became the principal operating base for the Loose route. Only one tram that worked this service could now be housed at Tonbridge Road Depot. Four trams earmarked for the Tovil route also shared the accommodation at this location.

This interesting transition from one mode of transport to another has been described in an article which appeared in *Motor Transport* on 18th March 1929:

During the period 1st May to 31st December 1928, the average operating expense per trolley bus mile was 12.751 pence, whilst the average revenue was 22.633 pence. The mileage amounted to 112,788, and the number of passengers to 1,597,298. Compared with the number of passengers carried on the trams on the same route during the corresponding period of the previous year, there is a significant rise of 21.2 per cent, clearly showing that the inhabitants are cultivating the riding habit and that they appreciate the new mode of transport.

Certainly, the carrying capacity of the trolleybuses is slightly greater than that of the trams, the figures being fifty-eight and fifty-four respectively. In addition, the upper decks of the trolleybuses are totally enclosed, whereas the trams were not. Actual running time on the round trip, High Street-Barming-High Street, has been reduced from the tram time of thirty-six minutes to thirty minutes. Until 11am a ten minute service is maintained, whilst after that hour the service is one of seven and a half minutes, except on Saturdays, when it is every six minutes throughout the day.

Parliamentary powers have been obtained to run trolleybuses on all three existing tram routes, and it is proposed to purchase eight more trolleybuses to replace the trams on No.2 route, from High Street to Loose – a distance of 2½ miles. Six wheeled vehicles have been chosen again, but the bodies will be single instead of double deckers.

The new service is scheduled to commence next August, and the whole of the town's tramway tracks will then be removed, as, at the same time, four Leyland single deck buses, now on order, will take over the remaining tram route No.3, from High Street to Tovil.

At a later date it is possible that trolleybuses will open a new route of 1½ miles on the Sutton Road to serve a garden city being built at Mangravet Wood.

This contemporary account makes it clear that the financial benefits of the conversion from trams to trolleybuses were encouraging. Journey times were also improved and, of course, in inclement weather top deck passengers were now protected from the elements. Although the members of the transport committee were familiar with the operation of single deck trolleybuses in Hastings, Ipswich, Southend and other places, there was no serious attempt to use such vehicles on the Loose route. They might have fitted the bill had the Tovil section been wired for trolleybuses; however, this line had never really paid its way and the safer option was to implement a motor bus route and connect it with an existing service to Hackney Road in the town.

Thus on 1st August 1929, the Tovil trams breathed their last, largely unmourned by the travelling public. At about the same time the council decided to press ahead with the trolleybus extension along Sutton Road. Although a matter of conjecture, the idea of economising by taking wiring, overhead equipment and poles from Tovil in order to recycle them on Sutton Road must have crossed the official mind. It is possible that this transfer took place, but documentary evidence is lacking.

Mill Street is closed, most probably for the tram rails to be lifted. English Electric trolleybus no.24 is depicted as it weaves its way through the traffic. It does resemble a free-for-all on the highway with an assortment of vehicles jostling for position.

Powers were obtained for a one way trolleybus wiring scheme in the town centre. Outbound vehicles would now descend Gabriels Hill and then traverse Lower Stone Street to Wrens Cross, where the inbound wiring diverged via Knightrider Street and Mill Street to return to the Cannon on High Street. In addition to overhead wiring crews being out on the road, the permanent way staff of the tramway department had one last, sad job to carry out. Pointwork was installed near the Wheatsheaf on the Loose Road. A siding was constructed to receive the tram fleet, no longer needed after the Tovil and Loose conversions.

Posed for a publicity shot, trolleybuses nos. 13 and 14 occupy road space on the approach to the Medway bridge. Tram tracks are in evidence, but the separate overhead wires necessary for the railed vehicles have disappeared. All this area was redeveloped in the 1960s to cater for new highways. *Dave Jones Collection*

The final day of tramway operation in Maidstone was 11th February 1930. Car 2 left the Cannon at 10.50pm, using tracks in the town centre for the last time. Under the control of Motorman F. Rose it reached Loose terminus and then trundled back to the scrapping siding at the Wheatsheaf. The choice of Driver Rose was particularly apt, as he had been with tramways since the opening in 1904. Another source states that a Mr. King was at the helm of the last car, which contained the Mayor and members of the council. Perhaps on the last run, several individuals had been 'on the handles' – tramway speak for the controller and the handbrake.

After the arrival of car 2, the siding was then full of redundant trams. One vehicle, car 14, did manage to escape a fiery fate. The Chatham manager, Mr Bousfield, on an official visit spotted the tram and decided to add it to his fleet, where it was renumbered car 52. In the event this tramcar only saw a few months service, because the whole of the Rochester, Chatham and Gillingham network was replaced by buses on 30th September 1930.

As the new day broke on 12th February 1930, passengers waiting at the Kings Arms, Loose were treated to a trolleybus ride into town, in place of the familiar open top tramcar. According to contemporary eyewitness accounts the Sutton Road extension to a turning circle in Grove Road was not ready for the big day in February. It is uncertain when this wiring was energised for public service, but it is possible that another five weeks elapsed before the system reached completion. Through services were instituted on a Barming-Loose-Barming-Sutton Road-Barming rotation.

An increase in the trolleybus fleet saw seven new vehicles delivered from English Electric; they received the numbers 23-29. They were similar in appearance to the original eight Ransomes, but were not as popular with the crews, who complained that nos.23-29 were less robust than nos.11-18. When first delivered, the new arrivals showed a tendency to dewire. This fault was traced to inadequate tensioning of the trolley springs and the matter was soon rectified.

Steam, electric and petrol driven vehicles are in evidence in this view of the High Street. Disused tramlines remain in the roadway. The motor age is in full swing. Advertisements for ARMSTRONG SIDDELEY – THE GO ANYWHERE CAR and for ROOTES – BUY BRITISH CARS are prominent. William Rootes founded his empire in 1913. In the following year he established his headquarters in Maidstone and by 1924 Rootes Limited had become the largest lorry and car distributor in the country.

Smoking was allowed on the top deck, so the chap looking suspiciously at the photographer will have to mount the stairs on trolleybus no.15. The Town Hall building is in the background.

Passengers generally benefited from the conversion to trolleybuses. Vehicles, such as no.18 seen here on Tonbridge Road, were more comfortable than the trams they replaced and offered more protection during inclement weather. The trolleybus in this view bears advertisements for KENT MESSENGER, the county wide newspaper, and for ROOTES. This latter informed the public that easy terms could be arranged for the purchase of a new motor car. Maidstonians were being urged to take to the open road now and pay later!

The system now settled down to a fairly uneventful existence. We get a glimpse into everyday operation from an account published in 1932:

One or two features of the system are unusual. For example, workmen and workwomen – in fact, all eligible to contribute to the National Health Insurance scheme – are qualified to apply for the issue of a token, production of which on a corporation vehicle entitles the owner to receive a half-price workman's ticket, any weekday up to 9am (the return half useable after noon), or between noon and 2pm.

Another interesting fact is that, to obtain the desired revenue rate per passenger-mile, whilst providing convenient stages, higher fares are charged on certain outward (uphill) journeys than on the inward journeys. Thus a yield of 1¼d is obtained by charging 1d inward and 1½d outward. The unexpected result is that more passengers ride inward, thinking they are getting a cheap fare.

The account goes on to list some financial statistics for the year ending 31st March 1931. The net profit on the trolleybus operation was £4,954, whilst the motor bus side of the undertaking recorded a loss of £3,677, thus leaving the corporation in credit by just over a thousand pounds. It was stated that the trolleybuses had carried 5,039,301 passengers and had run 401,187 car miles.

West Borough Maidstone is featured in early trolleybus days. We are looking away from the centre of town to observe two of the vehicles which supplanted the Barming trams. Tram tracks are still in evidence, therefore, we can assume that the Tovil and Loose routes have yet to be replaced. *Richard Stevenson Collection*

The reporter then described the work of the depot staff:

All the maintenance work for the two fleets (buses and trolleybuses) is undertaken at the Tonbridge Road Depot, at which the offices are located and all the vehicles are housed. A suburban car shed (Loose) which was in service has been sold, because the routes are not very long and it is desirable to centralize the control.

After 15 months service each trolleybus comes in for a complete overhaul, its licence being surrendered and a new licence taken out a month later, when it is ready to be recommissioned. Thus there is always one trolleybus in the shops. The month's work includes lifting the body and completely rebuilding the chassis, as well as stripping and reconstructing the body. All electrical and mechanical work is effected on the premises, including the winding of armatures and field coils.

Whilst the depot hands work early shifts (starting at 4am) and late shifts (finishing at midnight), no actual night work is undertaken, even for washing and inspection purposes. This permits better supervision of work.

During the 1930s the county of Kent witnessed the arrival of other trolleybuses in place of tramcars. In 1935 the towns of Welling, Bexleyheath, Erith, Crayford and Dartford were linked by London Transport routes 696 and 698. Trams still ran into central London from Abbey Wood and Woolwich. In the extreme west of the county the inhabitants of Penge could savour the new trolleybuses on route 654, which served Croydon and Sutton. However, the railless electric traction revolution failed to take hold in Gravesend, Sheerness, Rochester and Chatham, the Isle of Thanet, and at Dover. All these tramways were replaced by motor buses. Just over thirty miles from Maidstone the trolleybus system of Hastings in the neighbouring county of East Sussex, was quite extensive and eventually came under the control of Maidstone & District Motor Services. M&D had their headquarters in the town of Maidstone.

# 6 Consolidation

In the 1930s relations between the corporation and M&D were cordial. Neither saw the other as a potential competitor. The bus company charged a minimum fare of 4d for any service beginning in the town centre, whereas the maximum for travel on a corporation vehicle was 3d. Unfortunately, as we shall see, the relationship between Maidstone Corporation Transport and Maidstone & District Motor Services was not a marriage made in heaven. It would eventually deteriorate amid accusations of bad faith and duplicity.

At the end of the decade thoughts turned to route extensions and to modernising the fleet of the Maidstone network, small though it was. As regards serving new areas of the town, estimates were prepared for wiring to be erected as far as the Bull Inn, Barming. This hostelry was situated just outside the borough boundary. A new substation was built in anticipation of the work proceeding; however, events of the continent of Europe in 1939 would delay the project of implementing another Barming terminus.

In the case of the rolling stock, trolleybus design and reliability of equipment had advanced by leaps and bounds since the abandonment of the town's tramways. The Ransomes and English Electric vehicles now looked distinctly antiquated. The trolleybuses served natural traffic routes, were well patronised and popular with passengers. On the motor bus side of the undertaking expansion had been limited in the 1930s to new routes serving Queens Road (Malling Terrace), the Foster Clark Estate, Mote Park Estate and Holland Road.

Pictured in the 1940s, trolleybus no.26 still looks in fine fettle, if a little dated compared to contemporary designs. It is a fine summer's day as it climbs out of the town in the direction of Loose. Note the close spacing of the overhead wires.

An indication that more up to date rolling stock might be needed occurred on August Bank Holiday, 7th August 1939. In those days the statutory day off was fixed for the first Monday in August. True to a British tradition, it had been raining on the day in question! Driver Anderson lost control of his vehicle on the descent of Lower Stone Street. It skidded at Wrens Cross and overturned at the entrance to Knightrider Street. Thirty passengers were taken to hospital. At the subsequent enquiry, held on 11th August, it was ascertained that the driver attempted to turn left into Knightrider Street, when a more logical course of action would have been to risk dewirement, but remain upright, by plotting a course straight ahead at Wrens Cross. Doubt was also cast on the state of the tyres, which would not have gripped on the wet road surface. The vehicle involved, no.29, sustained damage and was repaired by Beadle Coachbuilders of Dartford at a cost of £175.

If the locals thought they had had enough excitement with the Wrens Cross debacle, they were in for a much ruder shock less than a month later, when war was declared. Frantic preparations had been going on in the three weeks leading to 3rd September. Air raid precaution measures involved most of the population. Vehicles had to conform with blackout regulations. Headlamps and interior lights were masked and anti blast netting was affixed to the windows. Platform staff and potential passengers had to adjust to the utter gloom of late evening and nighttime travel along streets with little or no illumination. Inevitably, it took some skill to negotiate the overhead points, known as frogs, and the section feeds situated at half mile intervals. Trolleybuses had to coast under these feeds. Application of power by the driver would result in arcing, which would be seen from enemy planes.

As it was, there was very little enemy activity in the skies over Maidstone, until after the fall of France in the summer of 1940. The Germans then had the benefit of airfields near the Channel coast, from which they could launch bombing raids on the Home Counties. Although there was a military presence in the area, as well as factories engaged in war work, it was mainly the civilian population in the firing line. Air raids began at the end of August and by the last day of October the town had suffered on eight occasions. On 'Black Friday' 27th September 1940, over fifty bombs dropped on the town with the result that twenty-three people lost their lives. On 31st October 1940, Mill Street and Knightrider Street were rendered impassable. The road surface was damaged and the overhead wiring brought down. It took several days to remedy the situation. In the meantime a single set of inbound wires from Wrens Cross via Gabriel's Hill to the Queen's Monument was erected as an emergency measure. This alternative diversion acquired more than a temporary status and lasted for the duration of war.

In the next two years cuts were made to services and certain bus stops were sacrificed in order to save fuel and to reduce tyre wear. Rubber became a precious commodity. The same could be said about the rolling stock. From 1942 onwards a dispersal programme of vehicles was instituted. Trolleybuses evicted from Tonbridge Road Depot found night time accommodation in the open on the verge by the Fountain Inn, Barming. The idea behind this was, of course, to minimise the impact of a direct hit on the depot and the associated loss of buses and trolleybuses.

The fleet was strengthened by the arrival of nos. 54 and 55 in the summer of

As an emergency measure during the Second World War a number of trolleybuses were kept overnight at this location by the Fountain Inn. Note the patriotic exhortation to save fuel in the home, so that vital war work could continue in factories. *Bill Haynes/Colin Barker*

Utility trolleybus no.54 arrived in 1943. Drivers were said to prefer the four wheelers over the members of the original fleet. The vehicle is depicted in the town centre in the early post war years. *C. Carter*

1943, to be followed the next year by nos. 56, 57 and 58. These wartime utility vehicles were the first four wheelers in the fleet. Each had a Sunbeam Type W chassis with electrical equipment by BTH. Bodywork was by Park Royal. Drivers indicated their preference for these trolleybuses over the more unwieldy three axle vehicles, which formed the rest of the fleet and were now showing their age. Therefore, a decision was taken to order ten new trolleybuses as soon as deliveries could be guaranteed in the early post war period.

Hostilities in the European theatre of war ceased on 8th May 1945. VE Day was celebrated across the country. In Maidstone during the Battle of Britain over two hundred bombs had fallen on the town; they caused fifty-three fatalities. VJ Day followed on 15th August, when the Japanese surrendered and the Second World War ended.

After the initial euphoria of victory had worn off, the country faced a long reconstruction period, often characterised as a time of austerity. On a local level the first of the changes concerned the General Manager of the Maidstone undertaking, A.T. Lambert, who asked to be relieved of his duties. He had been in harness since tramway days and had overseen a transformation in the provision of public transport for the town. His successor was C.S. Johnson, who took up his post on 1st January 1946.

Investment in the trolleybus system was near the top of the new manager's agenda. The Maidstone Corporation (Trolley Vehicles) Order Confirmation Act 1946 set out to extend the wiring from the Fountain to the Bull Inn, Barming. It allowed the corporation to borrow the sum of £3,667 to complete the works. At a public inquiry held on 15th April, objections by Kent County Council and Maidstone & District Motor Services were heard. Relations between the bus company and the corporation had cooled somewhat since pre-war days and they were about to get worse. In spite of these objections the Act was passed and the corporation's overhead wiring department went into action.

The new extension came in over budget at £4,155; this included the purchase of seventy traction standards. Some of the labour on the new turning circle was supplied by German prisoners of war. Public service to the Bull Inn began on 22$^{nd}$ May 1947. From the junction with Glebe Lane to the terminus the route was bounded by fields, orchards and hedgerows. The last few hundred yards of the extension lay outside the jurisdiction of the County Borough of Maidstone. A service pattern was now introduced: Bull Inn – Sutton Road – Fountain Inn – Loose – Bull Inn.

Modernisation of the fleet was also a priority. Twelve new trolleybuses had been ordered; the first of which arrived in September 1946. The final delivery was in April 1947. This influx of new blood into the rolling stock resulted in the withdrawal of ten of the original six wheelers. The remainder of the pre-war vehicles lasted another few months; they were disposed of to various individuals. Several members of the obsolete fleet escaped scrapping to become sheds or temporary living accommodation.

Some new ideas were put into practice as regarding short workings. These alterations to the timetable entailed the construction of turning circle wiring at the Cannon and at the Wheatsheaf. This latter facility saw only very restricted use, although the loop was always handy for emergencies. The Cannon loop was employed more intensively by Sutton Road shuttle services.

Further work for overhead linesmen included updating the wiring to conform to modern standards of a two feet separation between running wires. The previous norm of fifteen inches or eighteen inches was gradually replaced, as were most of the ex tramway fittings used in the 1930 conversion. An innovation by Assistant Electrical Engineer, C. Emby, was the use of curved segments of six or eight feet in length to ease trolley heads round sharp curves. These were successful in minimising dewirements and official visitors from other British trolleybus

Trolleybus wires reached Barming, Bull Inn terminus in 1947; Sunbeam no.73 was delivered to Maidstone in the same year. Here it is pictured awaiting departure for the Grove Road terminus on Sutton Road.

Trolleybus CBX 532 was purchased from Llanelli in South Wales. These vehicles were bought as a stop gap measure and they languished in the depot for some time before they were placed in service. No.83 has just passed the Wheatsheaf junction.
*Stan Letts*

operators were sufficiently impressed to employ them on their systems. Fittingly, these examples of overhead equipment were known throughout the industry as 'Maidstone Curved Segments'.

General Manager Johnson lasted until 1948, when he accepted an appointment with the Hong Kong tramways organisation. He was replaced by T. Bamford, previously in charge at Barrow-in-Furness Corporation Transport. One of his first duties was to formulate a strategy to sort out the financial affairs of the department. The trolleybuses made a profit, which was then eaten up by the loss making performance of the corporation's motor buses. Clearly, economies had to made. There was also pressure to raise fares in order to cover the deficit. It was therefore not surprising that a general fare increase occurred on 1st August 1949.

The adverse financial situation was beginning to show signs of improvement by the first year of the new decade. Trolleybuses still outshone their internal combustion engine brethren. The profit made by the former covered the losses of the latter, leaving a small surplus for the corporation. The Maidstone motor bus routes had to pay for themselves and it was with this in mind that the decision was taken to use this form of transport to serve the new Shepway Estate. It was once thought that trolleybuses were pencilled in for the estate, but subsequent research has revealed that this was never more than a pious hope by several members of the council. However, even if trolleybuses did not supply the internal transport needs, an extension of the Sutton Road service would cater for residents on the southern edge of Shepway.

Three cornered negotiations had been going on between the South Eastern Licensing Authority of the Traffic Commissioners, Maidstone & District Motor Services and Maidstone Corporation. The discussions took place in an atmosphere of mutual distrust and suspicion. Leaks to the press by sundry councillors, who suggested that trolleybuses might be welcomed at Linton Corner or indeed at Sutton Valence, deep in M&D territory, were not calculated to improve relations. Provocative statements such as these soured the whole proceedings and in modern parlance they were deliberate attempts 'to rattle M&D's cage'. There was no love lost between the two parties and it must be remembered that M&D had objected to the Barming trolleybus extension. The company had a reputation in the industry of vigorously defending its interests.

Matters came to a head in 1951, when proposed fare increases were vetoed by the Licensing Authority. It was suggested that public transport in Maidstone should be subject to economies and that these savings could be achieved by the elimination of unnecessary services. In short, a comprehensive co-ordination agreement should be hammered out between the two operators. Negotiations had also continued throughout this time on a takeover by Maidstone & District. The management team at the bus company were casting envious eyes on the routes operated by the brown and cream buses and trolleybuses; they reckoned they could do a better job and implied as much in the talks with the council. It was thus no surprise when in November 1951, the sub committee appointed to discuss the sale of the undertaking showed the representatives of M&D the door. The point was made forcibly that there would be no joint committee, no agreement to pool receipts and above all there was no evidence that the bus company could provide a better service!

Now that this unpleasantness was out of the way, planning continued for the future. For an outlay of a thousand pounds two second hand vehicles were acquired from Llanelli in South Wales. They were numbered 83 and 84 in the fleet; they left their native town in 1952, but it was some months before they appeared on the streets of Maidstone. As a balance to these arrivals there was a departure in July 1953. Mr. Bamford left to manage the Doncaster Corporation undertaking. His successor was Walter Kershaw, who had previously managed Colchester Corporation Transport.

# 7 Trolleybus Triumphant

On the General Manager's advice, the council voted to proceed with the Sutton Road extension. All the work was conducted in house. New poles and wiring were erected by the department's own overhead crew. An official inauguration by the Mayor took place on 21st June 1954. Trolleybuses ended their journeys by circumnavigating a traffic island at the entrance to Nottingham Avenue. Services conformed to the usual pattern of Barming, Bull – Nottingham Avenue – Barming, Fountain – Loose – Barming, Bull. During the week certain short workings were timetabled and on Saturday afternoons trolleybuses plied at hour hourly intervals between Grove Road and the High Street. No route numbers were allocated to Maidstone Corporation bus and trolleybus services.

We witness a wet day in summer at the Nottingham Avenue terminus on Sutton Road, not long after this section of wiring was opened. Trolleybus no.55 has just set down its passengers from town and the crew take a short rest before the trip back to Barming Fountain Inn. *Jim Joyce/Online Transport Archive*

Another view of Nottingham Avenue terminus; however, this time we are looking east. The road behind no.57 was the site of the last extension to Parkwood Estate. *Peter Mitchell*

On 14th July 1954, there was a celebration to mark fifty years of municipal transport in Maidstone. Trolleybus no.66 was suitably decorated with flags, bunting and coloured lights. It was joined on its tour of the town by motor bus no.77, which was also suitably adorned. Whilst the future of electric traction in Maidstone appeared secure, a significant announcement was made by London Transport earlier in the year. On 28th April, an official statement from 55 Broadway pronounced the death warrant for almost all of the capital's trolleybus system. Transport historians often maintain that this marked the beginning of the end for the trolleybus in Great Britain, but matters were not so cut and dried. The country's bus manufacturers such as AEC and Leyland did indeed sense rich pickings in the wholesale abandonment of electric traction on the nation's streets. Their public relations departments realised the power of advertising coupled with payment schemes which allowed transport undertakings to purchase diesel buses at advantageous rates. As we shall see, these tactics would eventually feature in the campaign to rid Maidstone of its trolleybuses.

The wisdom of retaining electric traction was illustrated by the fact that in the financial year 1954/55 the Maidstone trolleybuses made a profit of £8,033, while the motor buses recorded a loss of £11,680. Obviously, the revenue from the Shepway buses had yet to make an impact. Needless to say, increased fares came into operation on 25th September 1955 in an attempt to cover the shortfall to the department. Part of the deficit on the motor bus side can be explained by alterations to existing routes in order to serve new housing developments, which generated much extra mileage. In the first six years of the 1950s bus route extensions had encompassed London Road, Plains Avenue, Oxford Road, Westmoreland Road and Hatherall Road.

Congestion began to assume greater importance. At certain times of the summer and on Bank Holidays the volume of motor traffic passing along the main A20 trunk road caused jams in the town centre. It was common knowledge among motorists in South London that the earlier you left for a day at the coast, the more chance you had of avoiding the crawl through Maidstone! Practical suggestions for a by pass had been aired in the 1930s, but there the matter rested. However, a brief respite from overcrowded highways was granted in the first few months of 1957, when petrol rationing occasioned by the Suez crisis hit the motoring public. Fuel shortages also affected some local motor bus services.

Towards the end of the decade planning started on two major projects – the future A20(M) Maidstone by pass and the Parkwood Estate off Sutton Road. As regards the by pass, it was opened in two sections in December 1960 and September 1961. Along Sutton Road the council already had trolleybus powers from the 1927 Act as far as the borough boundary. Further powers were obtained in July 1958 to prolong the route into the new estate via a loop using Wallis Avenue West, Brishing Lane and Bell Road. Construction costs were kept down by the use of second hand materials; this included £1,826 spent on traction standards and overhead equipment. It was calculated that the council had thereby saved £3,250. In addition two trolleybuses were acquired from Brighton in February 1959. Officials from Maidstone also visited Hastings and they selected five vehicles from the former Maidstone & District fleet, which operated in the seaside town and along the coast to Bexhill and Cooden.

The sun is back out again at Loose and the trees give shade for intending passengers. What a pleasant spot this was for a trolleybus terminus! Catering for the thirsty traveller was the Kings Arms pub, just out of shot to the left of the picture. Stan Letts, who took this picture, confided in your author that he partook of some liquid sustenance there before returning to town. Sixty years after this photograph was taken, nothing has changed much apart from the demise of the trolleybuses. The tree is still there, but the phone box has been moved. *Stan Letts*

The North Downs form the backdrop to this view. As the chap on the racing bike could testify, it was quite a climb all the way to the Wheatsheaf. Former Llanelli trolleybus no.83 is working to the then new terminus of Parkwood, opened in May 1959. This particular vehicle was withdrawn in October 1960. *Peter Mitchell*

Parts of the Loose Road have been widened since trolleybus times. Back in the 1950s the thoroughfare was still recognisable from tram days. Indeed, the overhead wiring above no.67 has a definite tramway feel to it. Note the POLICE-FIRE-AMBULANCE call box next to the traction standard, which has a typical Maidstone fluted urn finial. *Peter Mitchell*

Former Hastings vehicle BDY 809 moved north after the closure of its home system. Repainted in Maidstone colours in 1959, it is seen here on the approach to Loose terminus before the wiring was altered to a clockwise configuration. *Peter Mitchell*

We are looking straight down the muzzle of the Crimean War cannon. A more peaceful era unfolds in the street as no.72 slows to the regulation five miles per hour to pass under the overhead frog. The Barclays Bank building in the background was once castigated as looking like a breakfast cereal packet with a waffle sticking out the top! *Peter Mitchell*

Sitting on the top deck front seat of a trolleybus descending Gabriels Hill was an experience not to be missed. Although the Maidstone system was small, it had plenty of changes of scenery. The Bull Hotel has been another casualty of the march of time and was vacant when these notes were being written. In this narrow shopping street, on the left just past the trolleybus, is the Golden Boot – a celebrated Maidstone establishment and a family shoe shop with an historic pedigree. *John Bishop*

Trolleybus no.54 was rebodied by Roe in 1960. Two women board ex Hastings no.85. Note the utility styled concrete bus shelter with the small brown and white Corporation Transport stop sign.

Another second hand bargain, ex Brighton no.51, does the tour of the Parkwood wiring in advance of the official opening. In spite of the weather there is much to cheer up the committed trolleybus enthusiast. It seemed at this time that Maidstone was going to buck the trend and retain electric traction on its streets. *John Meredith/Online Transport Archive*

The fact that Maidstone was able to benefit from the second hand market was due to abandonments elsewhere. A large part of the Brighton system closed on 24th March 1959, to be followed by the total closure of the Hastings network on 31st May. Earlier in the same year on 4th March, in stage one of the London trolleybus replacement programme, routes 654, 696 and 698 (the only ones serving parts of Kent) gave way to diesel buses. It would seem that other people's loss was Maidstone's gain. However, by this time the future was looking bleak for the British trolleybus and it was anybody's guess how long the county town of Kent could hold out against the national trend, even if it was reaping the reward of previously used vehicles and cut price overhead equipment.

In view of the increase in size of the fleet, the option of regaining temporary possession of the former Loose Road tram depot looked attractive. It would ease accommodation problems at Tonbridge Road Depot. The place was rented from June 1959 and thereafter functioned as a store for vehicles awaiting disposal or overhaul.

The circular route around Parkwood occasioned some interest from transport enthusiasts and professionals alike. The service via Brishing Lane opened on 4th May 1959. Brishing Lane itself had existed for many decades and it was incorporated into the new road layout. Wallis Avenue and Bell Road were born with the estate. It was noticeable that the trolleybus infrastructure was installed prior to the erection of much of the housing. Folk moving to the estate said they were reassured by a fixed track transport system. The presence of poles and wires appeared to have a psychological effect on many, who feared that moving out of the centre of town 'into the sticks' would make them feel more isolated. The frequent trolleybus service was reliable. In these respects the concept and execution of the estate was viewed very favourably in town planning terms.

On the rolling stock front nos. 54-58 were sent north to be rebodied by Chas. Roe of Leeds. Also in 1960 the two ex Llanelli vehicles were mustered out of service and both ended up at the breakers' yard. The updating of the fleet augured well for the future and this positive trend was bolstered by the news that the council had asked for further powers to extend the Parkwood service further into the estate. The Maidstone Corporation (Trolley Vehicles) Order 1962 paved the way for new overhead equipment to be installed in Wallis Avenue East and part of Bell Road. The official opening was in August 1963; the wiring in Brishing Lane was then removed. It was always intended that the loop should be extended further via Longshaw Road, Selby Road and Bicknor Road. Combined traction and lighting standards were erected at these locations and residents were informed that trolleybuses would arrive, when sufficient new housing had appeared.

Members of the overhead wiring crew were also busy during the year at Loose terminus, where the turning loop was altered to allow clockwise operation of vehicles entering the stand outside the Kings Arms. Another task allotted to the team was the installation of a siding in the layby by the Technical School in Tonbridge Road, thus enabling trolleybuses to avoid the main traffic flow.

Plans were being prepared to alleviate traffic congestion in the town centre and on the approach roads to the Medway Bridge. Although the loss of the A20 traffic had made a difference, there were still concerns about the rising number of cars and the provision of parking for shoppers. As with other conurbations in Britain, it was alleged that problems caused by too many motor vehicles could be solved by the construction of an inner relief road. Early in 1964 powers were sought for a trolleybus presence on Bishops Way, as the new road was called. Wiring was to be installed over the westbound carriageway used by vehicles heading for Barming or short workings to the High Street. The route along Mill Street was to be abandoned. Thus 1964 started on an optimistic note, but behind the scenes a plot was being hatched to scrap the trolleybuses.

Unencumbered by advertisements, the recent acquisition from the south coast looks splendid. The Maidstone livery was particularly striking especially in the bright sunshine. And of course in those days public transport vehicles were regularly cleaned. The driver of no.51 approaches the Wheatsheaf roundabout with caution.
*Mick Webber*

The driver of HKR 6 wrestles a hard lock on the steering wheel as he pilots his charge round the Fountain Inn turning circle. This manoeuvre also included a brief incursion into the pub car park. The car in the picture was just out of range; however, in those days no one was silly enough to leave a vehicle unattended in the way of a large, heavy trolleybus! This junction is now a lot busier and is controlled by traffic lights. *Mick Webber*

The last 'hurrah' for the trolleybus system was the installation of new wiring on Bishops Way. Here no.58 turns on a short working to High Street. In the background is one of the new Leyland Atlanteans in the fiesta blue livery. *Peter Mitchell*

# 8 The Final Flourish

Even as overhead wiring was being installed at Parkwood, the rumour mill started to function. It was suggested that some members of the transport committee were less than happy with the notion that the county town of Kent should be wedded to the trolleybus. The three nearest systems to Maidstone, at Hastings, Brighton and London, had gone to the wall in 1959, 1961 and 1962 respectively. In the Home Counties only Reading and Bournemouth appeared to offer any hope for the survival of railless electric traction. The trends in public transport seemed very clear to many in the industry and especially to those engaged in the manufacture of diesel buses. After all, they argued, why be tied to an outmoded fixed track system, when the motor bus could be flexible enough to respond to altered road layouts and new traffic objectives. This was music to the ears of elected members in council chambers across the country, where decisions had to be made on future routes and services.

At a meeting of the full council on 29th April 1964, the decision was taken to scrap the system. It was initially suggested that each trolleybus should be replaced by its diesel counterpart on a one to one basis. A time schedule of four years was contemplated to implement the abandonment decision. Some of the reasons underlining this change of policy were already well known among transport professionals. Aside from the usual accusations of trolleybus inflexibility, lack of spare parts, lack of trained maintenance personnel etc., there was a pressing need in Maidstone for a new depot to replace the cramped conditions at Tonbridge Road. The idea of wiring this new building for trolleybuses was obviously infra dig in the modern era of the 1960s.

The news was greeted with dismay by some, but it is fair to say most of the native population either voiced no opinions or concurred with their elected representatives. Among the enthusiast fraternity the decision to abandon was the signal for any number of individual and group visits to take multiple last rides. It is therefore no surprise that photographic coverage of the years 1964 to 1967 is extensive.

In the summer of 1964 the undertaking celebrated its Diamond Jubilee. Trolleybus no.66 again donned the mantle of festivity and, suitably decorated, it toured the streets. Motor bus no.14 performed a similar role. Quite understandably, this was a bitter sweet occasion for trolleybus supporters, as they realised that the next jubilee would be an all diesel bus affair.

An obvious consequence of the official change of heart was the cancellation of the enlarged terminal loop on Parkwood. Traction standards had already been planted; they then served as street lights for the neighbourhood. However, the diversion via Bishops Way went ahead. It was too late in the day to postpone this last extension and, fittingly, a number of silver painted traction standards added a final note of distinction to the condemned system. Public service under the new wiring commenced on 13th December 1964. Overhead wires in Mill Street and the turning circle at the Cannon were dismantled.

The Diamond Jubilee of the undertaking was celebrated in some style. Here on the Loose Road we view decorated trolleybus no.66. Notice that by this time the overhead wiring had been modernised thanks to the acquisition of material and spare parts from the second hand market.

After the wiring was altered at Loose, the approaching trolleybuses had to make a quick exit from the A229 on to the terminal stand. In October 1964 your author has partly lent out of the top deck window just before the previous occupant of the terminus departed. Note the details of the trolley springs and the stowing hooks above the rear window.

The Parkwood Estate is still taking shape as trolleybus no.71 makes its sedate way across the landscape. There was something reassuring about a fixed track transport system in an environment where many of the new residents had been rehoused away from family and friends. *Mick Webber*

Negotiations had been concluded with Leyland Motors with the result that a number of Massey bodied Leyland Atlanteans were ordered. These rear engine, front entrance vehicles were eminently suitable for what was then described as 'one man operation'. The notion of dispensing with conductors was already well established on the Continent of Europe and this trend was about to have a significant impact in the UK.

During 1965 the gradual withdrawal commenced, beginning with no.62 in April. Three more trolleybuses followed until November, when the initial batch of the Atlanteans made an appearance. It came as a surprise or downright shock to many, when they first beheld the latest addition to the local street scene. The buses sported a livery officially known as fiesta blue. Traditionalists imbued with the spirit of Maidstone brown or golden ochre turned their noses up at this 'civic vandalism', as they termed it. Cynics had a field day. Comments heard by your author at the time varied from the unprintable to the humorous. 'Wishy-washy, insipid and uninspiring' were some of the kinder epithets. One wag who thought that the new bus hue belonged on a bedroom wall, rechristened the colour siesta blue!

In the end, although opinions were divided in the town, the revised livery was here to stay, at least until the next transport reorganisation. As mentioned previously, the original intention was to substitute one diesel bus for each withdrawn trolleybus. The effect of all this was to run a mixed service during the week, when passengers took pot luck as to which vehicle turned up at their stop. On Sundays and Bank Holidays the fiesta blue fleet stayed off the road, leaving the trolleybuses to perform their duties in time honoured fashion.

We are on the approach to Parkwood just before the turning into Wallis Avenue. This is a classic study of a Maidstone trolleybus on a bright summer's day just over half a century ago. For many reading this book this picture will evoke very pleasant memories. *Mick Webber*

Another ex Hastings vehicle tackles the gradient past Maidstone West Station. Corralls were one of the largest coal merchants in the south east. This was at a time before widespread central heating, when domestic households burnt fossil fuels. Coal usually arrived by railway and was then transported in sacks on a lorry to individual addresses. *John Bishop*

The two ex Brighton vehicles were comfortable, robust and relatively speedy machines. Here we encounter no.51, as it accelerates past the riverside wharf of Smythe & Drayson Ltd. Maidstone market was held nearby and at times of flood some of the stock of the wood yard used to float away down the Medway. *John Bishop*

One of the hits of 1962 was the Bernard Cribbins song "The Hole in the Ground". Whether the chap digging said hole was humming the tune, as no.51 pulled away from the stop at the Wheatsheaf, we shall never know. We are left to admire a fair assortment of 1960s motor cars and fashions. Note the Neilsons ice cream and frozen food delivery van on Sutton Road. *John Bishop*

Unfortunately the weather did not hold for the photographer and here in Knightrider Street we observe the evidence of a recent rain shower. Trolleybuses conformed to a one way traffic scheme in this part of town. No.64 will soon turn to the driver's right in order to reach the new wiring on Bishop's Way – rather aptly named for the creator of this picture! *John Bishop*

# 9 Abandonment and Beyond

On a personal note, the author visited Maidstone on several occasions during the last three years of the system. In case there should be any doubt, even as a teenager I was a firm advocate of electric traction. The very idea of trolleybus abandonment appeared totally perverse to me, and, as we shall read later in this chapter, other officials of the council thought the same. By this time conductors were used to visiting enthusiasts getting on at the Bull, bagging the front seats on the top deck and then staying on board, crossing and recrossing the centre of town, until they came back to the Bull again! Another favourite was to observe the trolley poles from the back seat, by leaning back and peering upwards through the back window; invariably this activity would result in a crick in the neck. Whatever one's stance, the impression always was one of trolleybus efficiency. My abiding memory of a visit in October 1966 was of watching an ex Brighton vehicle, probably no.52, accelerating from the Wheatsheaf along Sutton Road and easily outpacing the following traffic. As the headquarters of the Kent Constabulary is also on this thoroughfare, it probably wasn't a good idea to exceed the 30 mph speed limit too often.

Certain short workings continued until the end of the system. Here at the former Grove Road terminus a trolleybus makes the turn, while the conductress operates the pull wire leading to the overhead frog. British Road Services is another name that belongs firmly to the past. The organisation had branches all over the country. Renamed the National Freight Corporation in 1969, it was privatised by the Thatcher government in 1982. *Mick Webber*

The conductress of no.89 has crossed Sutton Road to rejoin her charge at the Grove Road turning loop. Is that another trolleybus fan on the left of the picture? Meanwhile on the other side of the road the queue grows. One hopes the people haven't been turfed off no.89 short of their intended destinations. *Mick Webber*

No.64 is depicted on Wallis Avenue, Parkwood, near the junction with Wrangleden Road. Although many local authorities in the 1960s enthusiastically put up high rise flats, here the emphasis was on low density housing. *Mick Webber*

Tonbridge Road was quite narrow in places, which had restricted the tramways to a single track and loops layout. No.55 passes the Congregational Church at the corner of Bower Street. This area is still recognisable today, although the church was demolished not long after the trolleybuses left the scene. *Peter Mitchell*

In trolleybus days Upper Stone Street was two way, not the gyratory race track it is nowadays. The buildings in this area were a wonderful collection of architectural styles dating back centuries in some cases. The top storeys of several old houses had a marked lean towards the edge of the pavement. *Mick Webber*

Trolleybus no.55 starts the gentle descent of Tonbridge Road towards the Bull Inn terminus. In the background another trolleybus lays over outside the Fountain Inn. The Maidstone & District Motor Services bus stop in the foreground lists routes 7 and 33. Both services connected Gillingham with Tunbridge Wells. *Mick Webber*

Former Hastings trolleybus no.88 has crossed the borough boundary and is now in Barming proper. It can be argued that for the last few hundred yards until the Bull turning circle, it was intruding on Maidstone & District territory. The bus company was one of the objectors to the wiring extension from the Fountain to the Bull. *Mick Webber*

Trolleybuses circumnavigated the war memorial in Barming. This was the first sight of wires for motorists coming from Tonbridge on the A26. Trolleybus no.54 pauses before the return journey to Parkwood.

No.87 just by the wiring which led to the depot on Tonbridge Road. The terrace housing on the right was already well established when the first tramcar passed this spot. In typical British style the builder of those dwellings nearest the trolleybus has stolen a march on his neighbours by adding mansard windows to his stock. Note also the small front gardens in an age before this feature was sacrificed for car parking space. *Mick Webber*

The last full year of the Maidstone trolleybus system was 1966 – a time also remembered for a general election and a world cup win for England. There had been a steady trickle of trolleybus withdrawals. Vehicles often ended up as temporary residents of Loose tram shed, before they made the final trip to the breakers' yard. An account of the situation appeared in the edition of *Commercial Motor* for 18th February. After listing the perceived drawbacks of trolleybus operation in a piece headed *Maidstone Likes Its New Buses*, the writer, Norman H. Tilsley, praises the new Atlanteans, which he says cost over £7,000 each. He was particularly impressed by 'the brightness of the interior Formica trimming' and he found that the recently introduced light blue and cream livery had 'caught on' with the public – *O tempora, O mores!*

As the year drew to a close the electric fleet had been reduced to fourteen vehicles and early in 1967 there was a final delivery of the Leylands.

This is definitely one of your author's favourite photos. Mum and son quicken their pace to catch the trolleybus in the hope that the conductor won't ring the bell before they are safely on board. A corporation Leyland diesel bus completes the public transport scene outside the Fountain Inn. On the opposite side of the road is the Terminus Café at the corner of Terminus Road. The name of this thoroughfare celebrates the arrival of the first trams in 1904. Note the contemporary fashions. The boy is wearing short trousers and has a school cap on his head; the lady belongs to an era when almost every female you knew wore a skirt! *Mick Webber*

Trolleybus no.52 passes the Baptist Church in Knightrider Street. It has PRIVATE on the indicator blind and is probably on an enthusiasts' special. In the intervening years since trolleybus abandonment the neighboring buildings by the church have been cleared away. The bus behind the Ford Anglia is in the 'fiesta' blue livery adopted by Maidstone Corporation Transport in the mid 1960s. *John Bishop*

One hopes the driver of the car that collided with the new Leyland Atlantean did not sustain serious injury. Otherwise, this is definitely a case of 'schadenfreude' for any true trolleybus aficionado! The German word means having fun at someone else's expense. A traffic policeman is already on the scene – no hi viz jackets in those days. *Peter Mitchell*

This picture needs but few words. The ceremonial last trolleybus enters the depot. It was a sad occasion. *John Meredith/Online Transport Archive*

Critics of the trolleybus were quick to accuse it of being wire bound and therefore inflexible in traffic. Whilst the zebra crossing outside the Cherry Tree in Tonbridge Road is being repainted, two trolleybuses confound their detractors by passing round an obstruction with relative ease. It is late October 1966 and the electric vehicles have only a few months of life left. *Richard Grover*

To cut a painful story short, the council announced that the system would close on 15th April. Trolleybus no.72 was decorated for the occasion and it toured the streets in the last week. On official instructions it did not carry any passengers. This ban was lifted for the final run, when it carried a civic party. The last act commenced at around 11.30pm at the High Street and concluded at the depot a quarter of an hour later. A reception was held in the transport offices, where the invited guests were treated to the usual valedictory speeches associated with this type of occasion. Whether anyone was so moved as to utter the phrase *sic transit gloria mundi* is not recorded. The fight to retain electric traction had been lost, and there our story comes to a conclusion. No.54 preceded it immediately so as to carry everybody.

At least, that is where this narrative should have ended, were it not for a chance encounter some years after the abandonment. As an invited guest, the author was attending a function run by a nationwide charitable organisation. The event in question took place at the Congress Theatre and Conference Centre, Eastbourne in October 1982. I fell into conversation with a gentlemen who was a retired civil servant. He had worked with Kent County Council at Springfield in Maidstone, before taking a position with the local authority. I received the impression he was a life long resident of the town. When I mentioned my visits to the area, the talk turned to the fate of the trolleybuses. He had strong views and said: "That was a bad decision, because the system could have lasted at least another decade, if not longer. I don't have much respect for the individuals who axed the trolleys. They wasted a valuable asset to the town".

I was intrigued. I wanted to know more. He then gave his account of the last few years of the system, based on conversations he had had and on documents he had seen. As he jokingly remarked, he didn't believe he was subject to any oath of 'omertà' (the Sicilian oath of silence – the film and book *The Godfather* were very popular at the time), when it came to talking about his former employers! His narration shed light on the workings of the transport department.

It seems General Manager, Walter Kershaw, in private conversations was quite vocal about the mental capacities, or lack of them, of his political masters. This wasn't a party political matter, in the sense of Tory/Labour/Liberal, more it was a case of certain individuals and their behaviour. The narrator was of the opinion that Mr. Kershaw was in favour of keeping the trolleybuses, but he had been pressured to follow the party line about the alleged inflexibility of the system.

In the early 1960s after the acquisition of second hand vehicles and sundry overhead wiring materials, the belief grew amongst some in the department that Maidstone could really benefit further from other abandonments across the country. At minimal cost they could pick up vehicles and equipment at bargain prices. In pursuit of this policy in the summer of 1961 the narrator was asked to visit the West Midlands. He had informal discussions with representatives from Wolverhampton and Walsall. The management in the former town had just announced an abandonment scheme. Enquiries were made about the condition of that corporation's newest vehicles. Walsall, on the other hand, appeared to have mapped out a survival strategy that could serve as the model for Maidstone.

Had this approach been followed up, then the course of history could have been changed. As it was, my informant sitting opposite me was scathing about the way Leyland Motors and their local agent 'wined and dined' certain individuals in order to obtain influence in the council chamber. He further alleged that a discounted payment schedule made the purchase of the Atlanteans an attractive proposition.

My conversation partner was convinced that there was enough serviceable second hand material on the market in the mid 1960s to cope with any road alterations or extensions to a new depot. He then ended by saying that he had no faith in the present (1982) management of the bus network.

It must be stressed that any suggestion of 'dodgy dealing' or 'creative accounting' is an unsubstantiated allegation. There appears to be no paper trail to support the idea that Leyland Motors acted corruptly. Half a century after the events it is unlikely that any evidence remains to be uncovered. As regards the purchase of the replacement buses, it was common practice in the motor industry to offer deferred payments to customers. However, the suspicion remains that all was not as it should have been; my informant was firm in his belief that a form of bribery and corruption had taken place.

His remark about the running of the 1982 transport undertaking was quite prescient. In order to comply with the provisions of the 1985 Transport Act, Maidstone Borough Council set up a company which traded under the name Boro'line. This organisation declared a large loss in 1989 and poor financial results later forced the company into administration in February 1992; it went out of existence in May of the same year. Thus we write *finis* to our story.

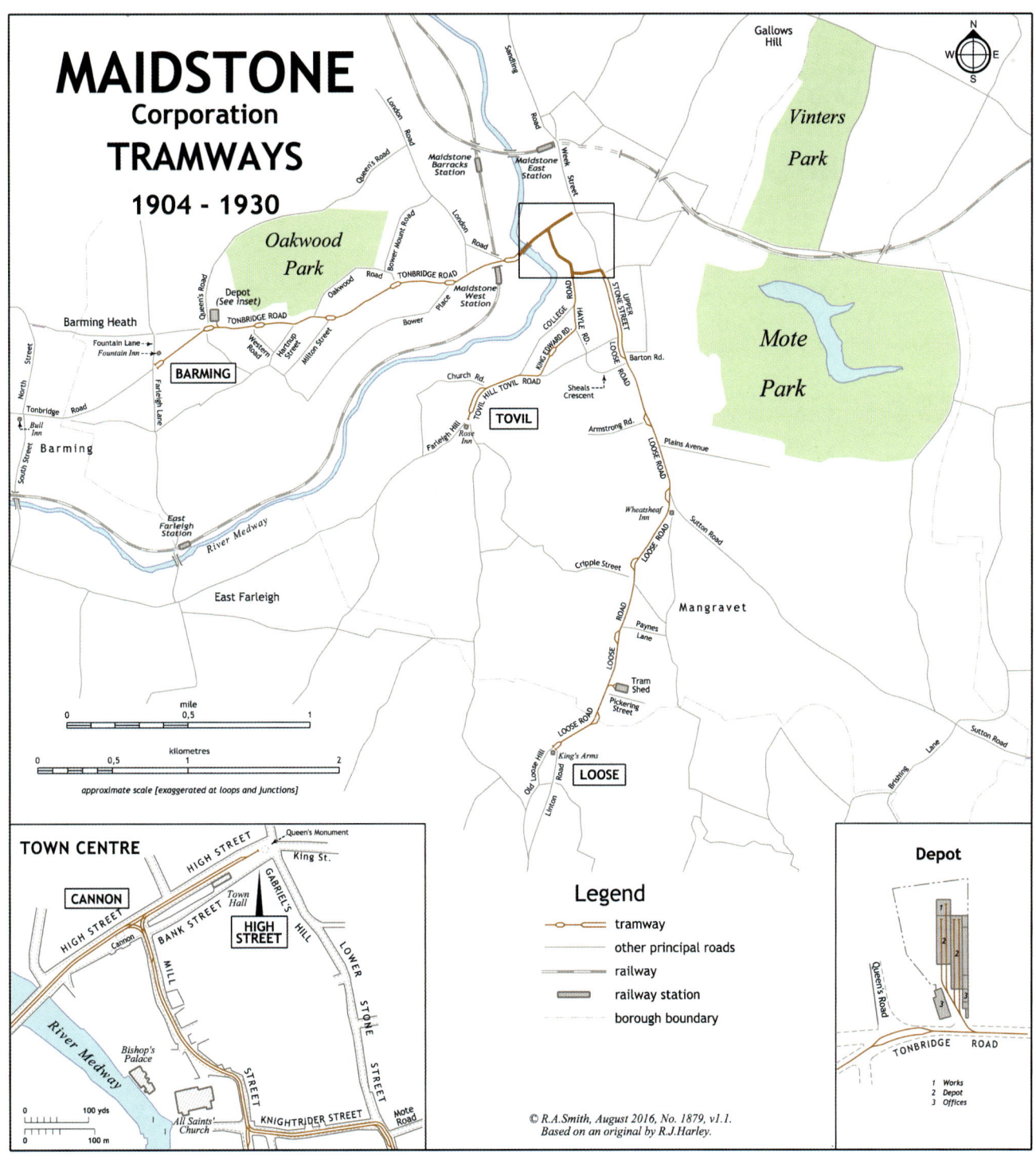

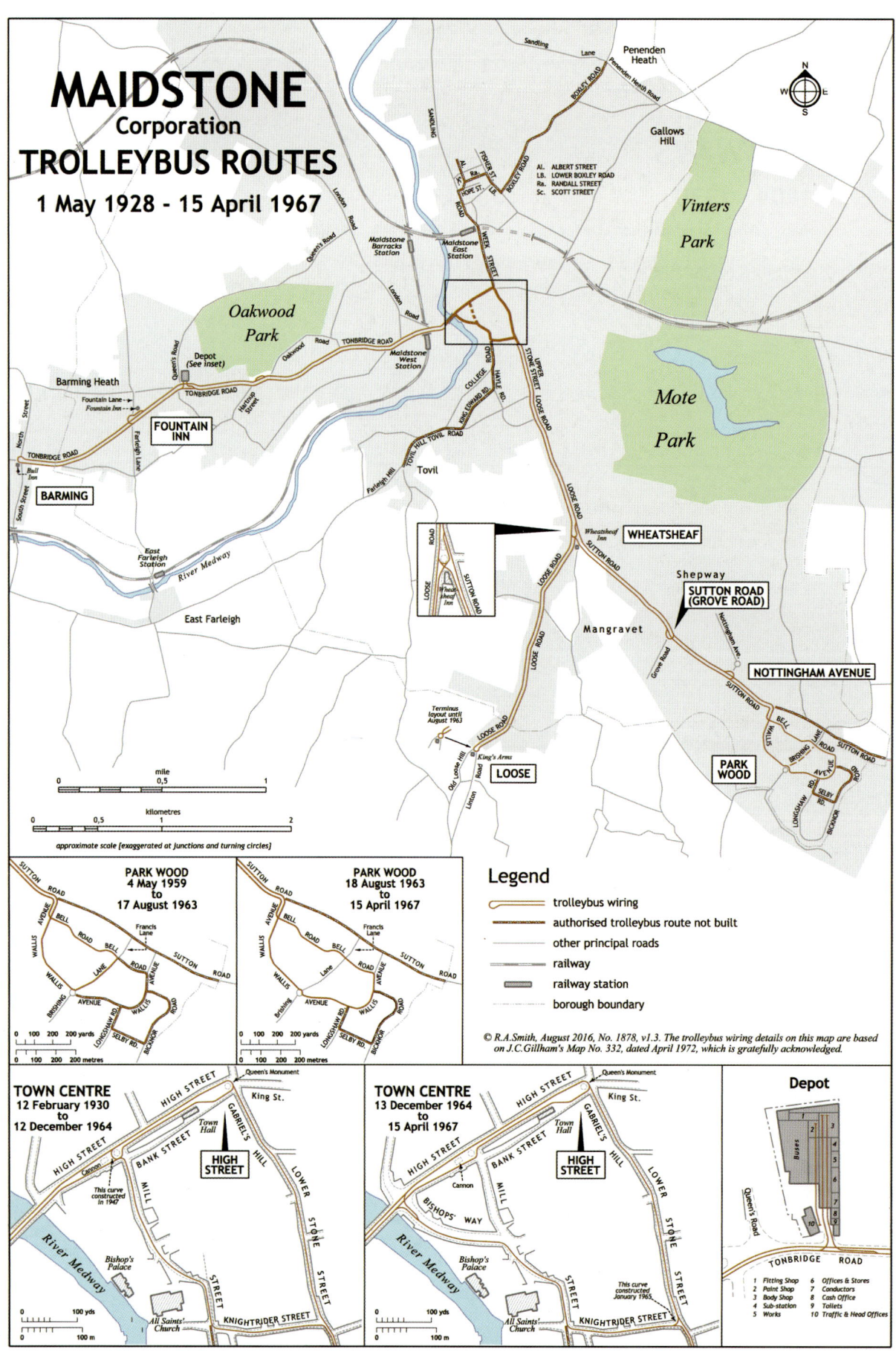

# Maidstone Tram and Trolleybus Chronology

### LEGEND

- new tramway
- tramway in operation
- tramway closed
- new trolleybus route
- existing trolleybus route
- trolleybus route closed

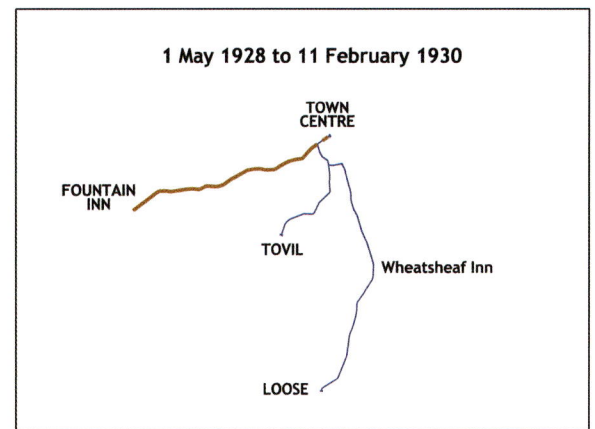

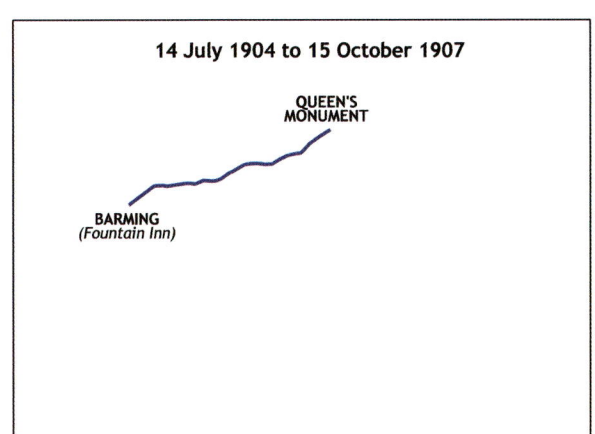

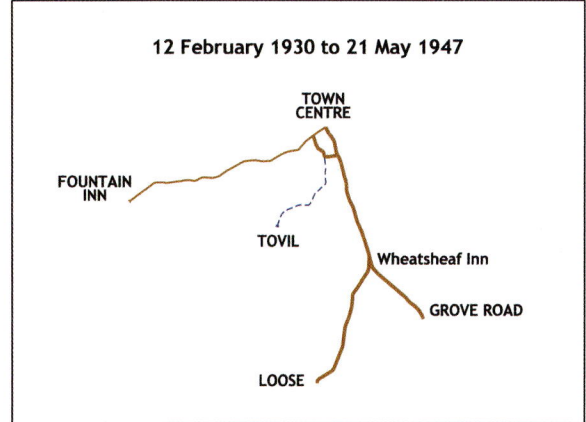

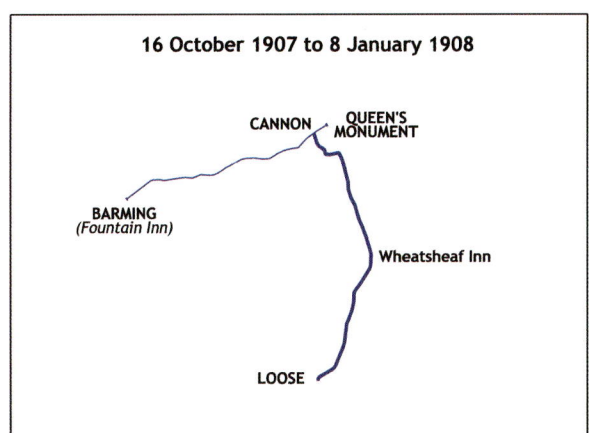

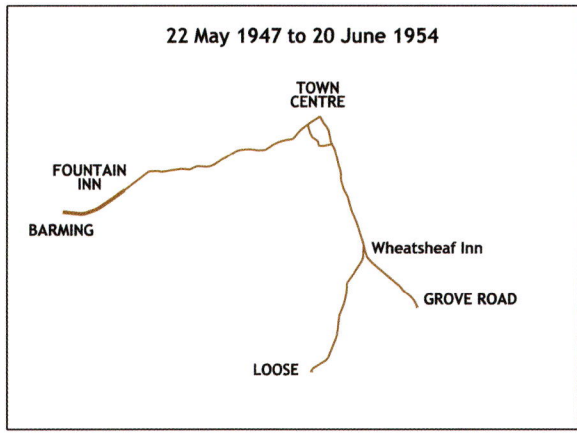

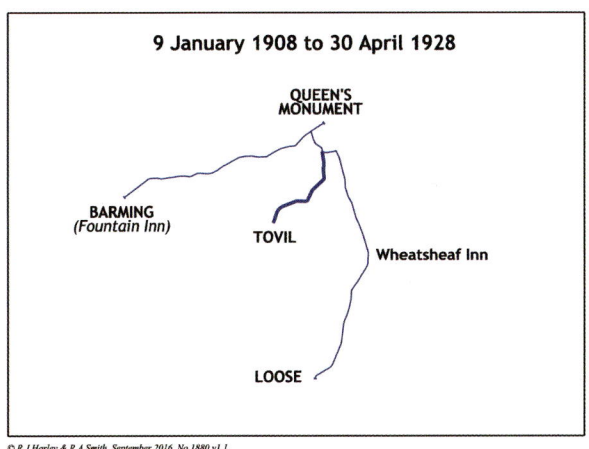

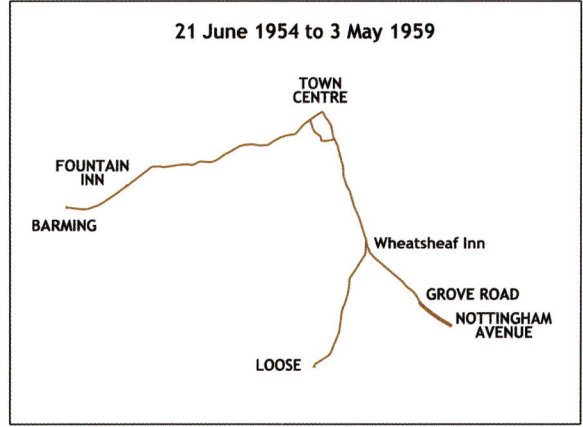

© R.J.Harley & R.A.Smith, September 2016. No.1880,v1.1.

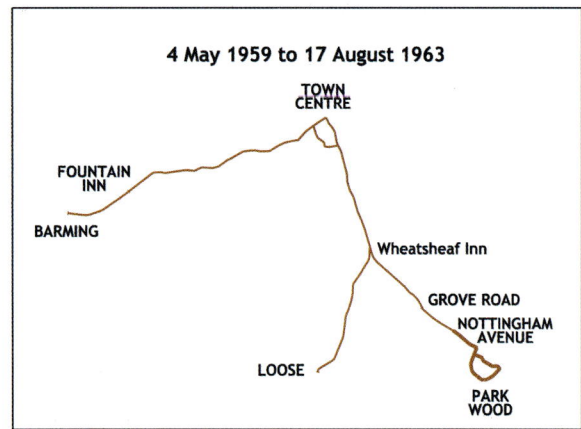

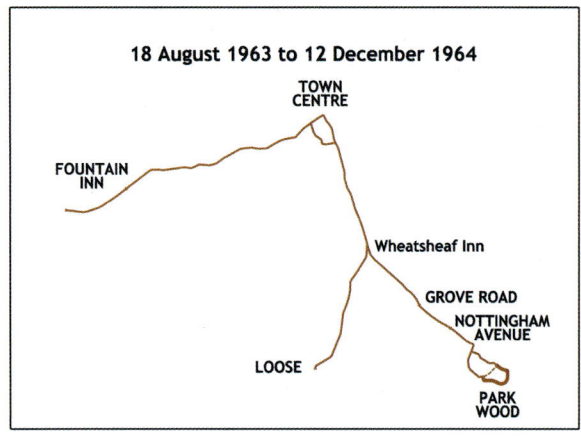

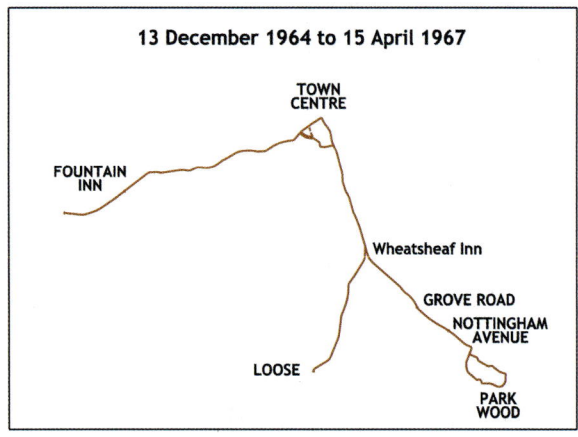

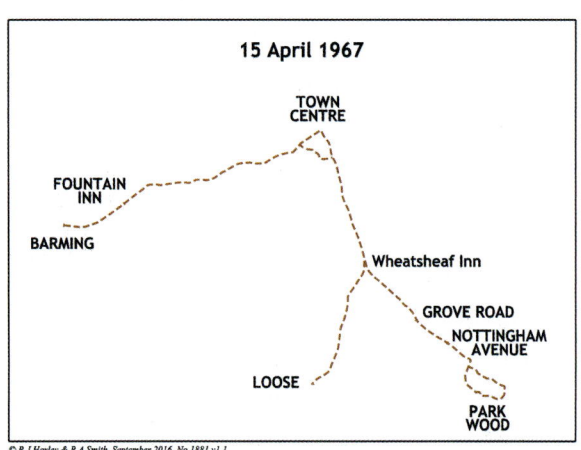

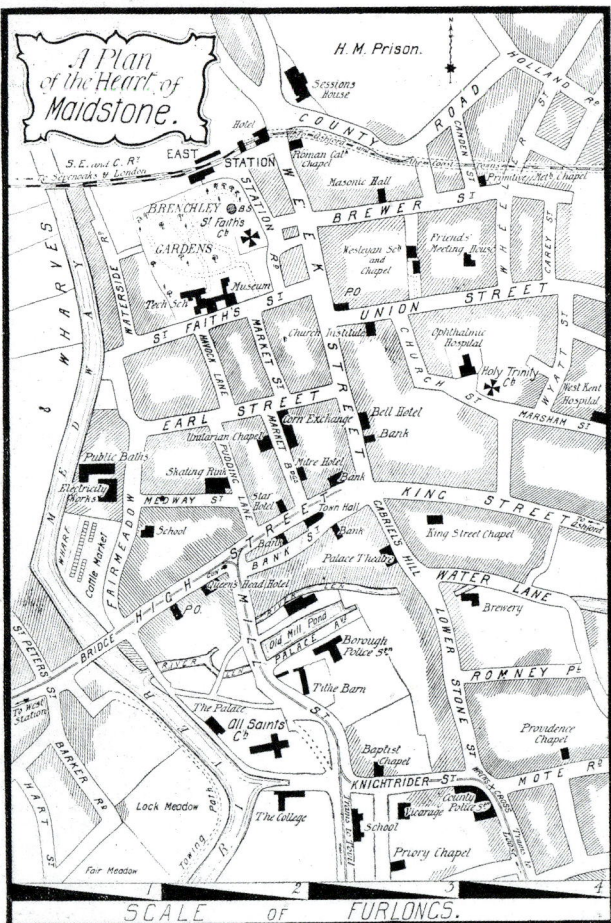

*Above* This rare map of central Maidstone appeared in an Edwardian guide book. It shows clearly the tramways and the principal buildings of the town. Much has changed in the intervening century. *Author's collection*

# Appendices

## Livery

When electric trams first appeared on the streets of Maidstone, they represented civic pride. Their smart appearance was enhanced by a very pleasing style of livery. Each vehicle entering service every morning was cleaned internally and externally; sending out an unwashed or soiled tramcar on to the streets constituted an unpardonable sin. Heads would roll among the depot staff if this ever happened.

The official livery of the trams was described as golden ochre and off-white. Throughout the history of electric traction in Maidstone the predominant colour of the vehicles was brown – be it light brown, mid brown, dark brown or even 'milk chocolate brown'. An expert in this field, Geoffrey Baddeley, in conversation with your author, remarked that the original tram livery was a very light brown, but this pigment was altered over time and took on a greenish, khaki tone. Although Geoff did praise the quality of early twentieth century paints, he acknowledged the effect of wear and tear, plus the annual varnish of each tramcar. This ageing process gave a gradual darkening of the brown livery.

As regards each individual tramcar the paint scheme was as follows:

Light brown/golden ochre: dashes, stair bands, cant rails, waist panels.
Off-white: window frames, top deck decency panel, rocker panels.
Red oxide: truck sides, trolley mast, lifeguards, hand rails.
Varnished natural wood: opening top lights, destination boxes.

The ochre painted parts of the car were lined in gold, while the lining on the off-white was black. The name of the undertaking MAIDSTONE CORPORATION was painted on the rocker panels in gold, shaded red; the same combination of colours was used for the fleet number on each dash. The town's coat of arms was displayed in the middle of the waist panels.

The water car appeared in an unrelieved golden ochre livery with the name of the undertaking in gold lettering on each side of the tank. A coat of arms was also displayed.

In later years the name A.T. LAMBERT was picked out in black letters on the bottom right hand corner of the rocker panel. It appeared above the words GENERAL MANAGER & ENGINEER.

A similar livery was adopted for the trolleybuses, although the lining was altered to dark green and brown. The name of the undertaking remained as before in gold lettering, shaded red. The town's coat of arms was changed in 1949; however, it took a few years for the new device to be applied to the sides of the trolleybuses and motor buses. To the casual observer it was difficult to tell the difference between off-white and cream, especially when several coats of varnish had been applied. Various minor variations in shades of brown were tried until 1953, when 'milk chocolate brown' made a brief appearance. Further changes occurred in 1954-56 when the short lived ginger brown and cream was replaced by the more traditional golden ochre. This distinctive colour scheme remained on some corporation diesel buses after trolleybus abandonment. It finally gave way to fiesta blue in November 1968, when the last diesel buses were repainted.

# Rolling Stock – Tramcars

**Cars 1-6**
Built by the Electric Railway & Carriage Works at Preston, Lancashire and delivered in May 1904, these trams were constructed to a very traditional British design. The lower saloon was furnished with longitudinal bench seats for twenty-two persons. A strip of red carpet served as the rather Spartan upholstery on each bench. Maroon curtains were hung at the windows Six electric lamps provided the internal lighting. Entry to the lower saloon was by means of a single sliding door at each end of the car.

Passengers gained access to the top deck by means of a quarter turn staircase. On the upper deck there was seating for twenty-six people. Single and double 'garden' seats with backs that could be flipped over according to the direction of travel were laid out in a staggered 2 & 1 arrangement.

The main dimensions were as follows: length of lower saloon sixteen feet, width six feet three inches, height six feet nine inches, overall length of car twenty-seven feet eight inches, height of car from rail level to top of upper deck railing thirteen feet three inches.

Current collection was by conventional trolley pole. Trolley ropes were attached to American style trolley retrievers, which were clipped on to the dash of each car. Although popular in North America and in other parts of the world, these devices never caught on in the UK. They were designed to prevent a dewired trolley pole from springing upwards from the overhead and thereby causing damage to itself and to the wiring.

Power passed from the overhead wire via a fixed head trolley wheel attached to the usual British trolley mast for open top cars. The trolley pole could only be turned in one direction. A cable then led to two Dick, Kerr DB1.C controllers before reaching the two DK.25B motors, each rated at 25 hp. Trams rode on a Brill 21E truck of six feet wheelbase, with a wheel diameter of thirty inches. Track gauge was three feet six inches. Each vehicle was equipped with Peacock hand brakes, together with rheostatic and Spencer track brakes.

An extra vehicle, car 7, was added to the fleet in February 1905. It was identical in design to the initial batch. As has been mentioned in the text, after about three years in service a number of alterations were made to these tramcars. The fixed head trolleys were replaced by the usual British swivel head variety. Automatic trolley retrievers were replaced by the conventional trolley rope. Headlamps were moved from the canopy to the dash. Indicator blind boxes, lacking in the original design, were placed above the upper deck rails, but were later moved to a position under the canopy and above the driver.

On closure of the Tovil route a number of trams from this batch were withdrawn and it is recorded that cars 1, 2, 4 and 6 survived until the end of the system in February 1930.

**Cars 8-17**

Built by United Electric Car Company at Preston, cars 8 – 15 were delivered in July 1907. Cars 16 and 17 followed in December. These tramcars were very similar to the original batch. They also had indicator boxes placed successively in two different positions. One important difference lay in the length of the lower saloon. This measured thirteen feet, giving an overall car length of twenty-four feet eight inches.

These were George Gundry's 'short' cars. After the demise of the Tovil service four trams from this batch were withdrawn. The rest soldiered on until the end of the system. Car 14 was sold to Chatham and received the number 52 in that fleet. It survived the Chatham abandonment in September 1930 and spent a third career as a shed on a farm at Lidsing, south of Gillingham.

**Car 18**

Built by UEC at Preston and delivered in 1909, this small single deck tramcar was known as a demi car. It was designed for operation by a single person, unlike the rest of the fleet, which required a motorman and a conductor. The operator of car 18 performed both these functions. Passengers boarded at the front and then paid the driver. The main dimensions were as follows: length of main saloon eleven feet, length over platforms twenty-one feet six inches, width six feet two inches.

Car 18 was mounted on a four wheel 21E type truck, manufactured by Mountain & Gibson of Bury, Lancashire, of five feet six inches wheelbase. Electric motors were by Raworth as were the 'R' series controllers.

In tramway terms this vehicle had a remarkably short life of just over one decade. It was retired from the Tovil route in 1919; it was later placed in the depot and basically forgotten about. It is probable that it did emerge on odd occasions until around 1926, when it remained inside Tonbridge Road Depot until disposal in 1928. Just over four decades later it was discoved in Winchelsea. The body of the car had been serving as a holiday bungalow. Rescued for preservation, car 18 was transported to Dover Transport Museum. Unfortunately, the restoration project failed and the tramcar was then dismantled.

**Water Car**

It was common practice for tramways to possess a works vehicle, which could water the streets in summer and keep the dust down. Edwardian highways were paved to varying standards and they were often plagued by the detritus of horse drawn traffic. This four wheel tramcar was equipped with a 300 gallon water tank. In order to clear the tracks in winter a revolving snow broom was fixed at either end of the vehicle. It was used until the early 1920s and was scrapped around the middle of that decade.

Other sundry rail vehicles included a flat truck and a hand propelled rail grinder used for trackwork in conjunction with welding apparatus.

Car 5 is photographed shortly after delivery to Maidstone. This pristine state did not last long, because the town fathers thought it might be a good idea to gain extra revenue by using their tramcars as mobile advertising hoardings.

Car 5 reappears in its final condition. The indicator box is placed above the driver's platform and the headlight has been fixed on the dash. Maidstone was one of the few operators who actually let spaces on the stair risers for commercial purposes. Local firm Grants was quick to seize the opportunity. Note the destination board BARMING & HIGH ST. The two other boards in use were TOVIL & CANNON, LOOSE & CANNON. *Dave Jones Collection*

Car 15 was one of the second, shorter batch of vehicles supplied for the opening of the Tovil and Loose routes. It is pictured at the depot in its final state. Obviously, motormen had to be hardy types to perform their duties on a platform exposed to the elements. Maidstone trams were unusual in their time by having direct quarter turn stairs to the upper deck. *Dave Jones Collection*

We observe the demi car 18 at the depot. Here it languished for some years with no real role in the day-to-day working of the tramway. However, this small tramcar did pioneer the concept of a single crew member responsible for collecting the fares and driving the vehicle. This is an idea which has since found almost universal favour in the world of public transport. The mechanical device on the left of the picture is one of a number of jacks used to separate tram bodies from their trucks. *Dave Jones Collection*

A miniature replica of demi-car 18 was constructed by Ron Leach of the Tramway and Light Railway Society. This fine working model in 1:16 scale displays the Maidstone golden ochre livery in all its splendour.

This three quarters of an inch to a foot scale model is electrically powered like the prototype from overhead wires with the current passing through the trolley wheel and trolley pole to the motors. Twenty-four volts suffice for the model in the picture; 500 volts DC were needed to operate the real thing.

# Rolling Stock – Trolleybuses

### Nos. 11-18. Registered KO 8891, 8543-4, 8892-8896

Chassis and bodywork built by Ransomes, Sims & Jefferies of Ipswich. These six wheel vehicles fairly represented the state of the art, when delivered to Maidstone in 1928. They made a favourable impression on General Manager Lambert, as he wrote in the edition of *Tramway & Railway World* for 12th July 1928:

In the design and construction of these vehicles particular attention has been paid, first and foremost, to the comfort and convenience of the passengers, and in many respects they are the most luxurious vehicles of their type that have yet been constructed.

The body was constructed by Messrs. Ransome, Sims & Jeffries Ltd., to accommodate 63 passengers, 31 in the lower and 32 in the upper saloon. All the seats are of the semi-bucket type, upholstered in antique brown shade real leather, the backs of the seats being covered with moquette. The seating is liberally arranged, with ample knee room between the seats, all of which are fitted with spring backs, except those over the wheel arches. The ventilation of the two saloons was made a special point in the specification. The lower saloon is fitted with six drop windows, operated by Rawlings' patent method. The ventilators are hinged under the cant rail and held in position by a non-rattle fixture.

The upper saloon has five drop windows on the sides and another in the front bulkhead. Three "hit and miss" ventilators are also fitted in the front bulkhead of the upper saloon. The internal finish is carried out in a most pleasing manner, the mouldings and panel work being finished in a rich mahogany shade, whilst the roofs of both saloons are white enamelled. The entrance to the vehicle is at the rear and consists of a very wide single step, about eleven inches from the ground, leading to a spacious platform. The staircase to the upper saloon is rather wider than the average and is fixed in such a way as to give a most convenient approach to the upper saloon.

A notable departure from usual practice is the method of carrying the trolley booms on the roof of the upper saloon, which has been patented by the makers. It is claimed, by this means, that the roof is relieved of the heavy stresses and strains, and transfers them directly to the pillars, which form the main stay for the sides of the bodywork. The construction forms a brace and thereby strengthens the roof, while permitting it to be made lighter than is usual. The pillars and hoop sticks supporting the roof and floors are reinforced with steel flitch plates. The body is thus strengthened by means of a series of steel bands completely encircling it.

The chassis is of the six wheel type, mounted on 40in by 8in pneumatic Dunlop cord tyres. The braking of the vehicles is somewhat out of the ordinary in that each vehicle has no less than twenty brake shoes. All wheels have brakes fitted. There is an independent brake on each of the six wheels, actuated by the Westinghouse air system. The same shoes can be operated at will by means of the ordinary foot pedal placed in the driver's cabin. The arrangement is such that, if required, the air pressure can be supplemented by foot pressure from the driver.

The four rear wheels have also an entirely independent set of brakes, operated by a hand lever. The writer, when drawing up the specification, was most anxious to make the vehicles as nearly fool proof as possible, and to avoid any chance of a driver (who may have previously driven an omnibus fitted with a clutch) making the mistake of suddenly depressing his controller pedal in an emergency stop, had the hand brake lever electrically connected with the controller circuit, so that when this set of brakes comes into operation the current is cut off. This, in practice, has worked exceedingly well. The braking system is excellently designed and gives good results.

The chassis is fitted with the Thornycroft patent bogie, which has many advantages, the most important of which is, perhaps, the fact that the torque reactions, due to acceleration and braking forces, are taken care of without the need for rigid torque rods.

In these omnibuses a third differential has been embodied for the driving of the rear axles, equalizing the drive between all four rear wheels, each of which is free to roll freely on the road at a speed which may differ from any of the others, due to varying diameters of tyres and other causes. The manufacturers are strongly of opinion that the fitting of a third differential will materially increase the life of the tyres, and tend to reduce power consumption under town service conditions.

The electric motors are of Ransomes, Sims and Jeffries' manufacture and are of the twin type, having two armatures mounted in a common casing, the horse power being 60/65. As the district is somewhat hilly, and the omnibuses have to run in dense traffic at times, series-parallel control was adopted. The acceleration is smooth and the vehicles are capable of good speeds on gradients of 1 in 15. The controllers are of the Electro-Mechanical Brake Company's manufacture. The steering is of special design, having a double reduction gear giving easy control, whilst the column is raked at a comfortable angle. A deviation indicator is fitted immediately in front of the driver.

We can glean from this description that the initial fleet of trolleybuses marked a distinct improvement on the trams they replaced. It only needs to be noted that each vehicle had its two trolley poles mounted on a single Estler base. This allegedly allowed greater flexibility over the conventional two trolley bases. Backing these trolleybuses out of the depot was adjudged easier with this system. Each vehicle cost £2,005.

Service ended for this batch after the Second World War. They were retired in 1946/7. Six trolleybuses were sold to A. Gilfrin, who later resold them as caravans or holiday homes. Two went to Sir Garrard Tyrwhitt-Drake for staff accommodation at his private zoo near Maidstone.

**Nos. 23-29. Registered KR 351-357**
Chassis and bodywork built by the English Electric Company. Delivered to Maidstone in 1930, each member of this batch cost £2,034-10s. Seats were provided for thirty on the top deck and for twenty-six people in the lower saloon. They were fitted with a single trolley base similar to that used by the initial group of Ransomes vehicles. The English Electric twin type motors developed eighty horsepower.

In appearance these trolleybuses resembled nos. 11-18, with the obvious exception that the driver's cab had a sloping windscreen, suggesting an early attempt at streamlining. The front panel of the upper deck was also set at an angle. Crews tended to prefer the Ransomes to the English Electrics. It was alleged that this latter batch did not handle as well and they felt more light weight and less substantial than the Ipswich made products. Nos. 23-29 were disposed of in 1946/7.

**Nos.54 and 55. Registered GKN 349, 380. Nos.56-58. Registered GKP 511-513**
Built by Sunbeam Commercial Vehicles of Wolverhampton and delivered to Maidstone in 1943/4, these four wheel vehicles had electrical equipment by BTH. Built to wartime utility specifications with bodywork by Park Royal. Seating was for thirty on the upper deck and for twenty-six in the lower saloon.

They possessed carbon skid inserts in the trolley head as opposed to the traditional trolley wheels of the earlier members of the fleet. In 1960 they were sent to Charles H, Roe of Leeds for rebodying in a more modern style. After they returned to their home town, they lasted until the end of the system in 1967.

**Nos. 62-73. Registered HKR 1-12**
Built by Sunbeam in 1946/7, these type W vehicles again had electrical equipment by BTH. Bodywork was by Northern Coachbuilders with seats for thirty on the top deck and for twenty-six on the lower. Nos. 62, 63, 67, 69, 70, 71 and 73 were withdrawn from service in 1965, the rest soldiered on until the last year of operation.

**Nos. 83 and 84. Registered CBX 532, 533**
Type W chassis by Karrier Motors, with utility style bodywork by Roe, these two trolleybuses were delivered in 1945 to Llanelli in South Wales. On abandonment of that system in 1952, they were acquired by Maidstone, but did not appear in service until 1955. Seating was the standard 30/26 split as regards upper and lower decks.

Never more than a stop gap in Maidstone, they were both withdrawn in 1960.

**Nos. 51 and 52. Registered LCD 51, 52**
Built new for Brighton Corporation and entering service in 1952, these two trolleybuses had bodywork by Weymann on a type 9611T chassis by British United Traction. Electrical equipment was by Allen West and Crompton Parkinson. Surplus to requirements after the first stage of trolleybus abandonment in Brighton, they were purchased by Maidstone in 1959. No. 51 was taken out of service in the summer of 1966 and its sister vehicle followed the next year at the end of the system.

**Nos. 85-89. Registered BDY 807, 809, 810, 817, 818**
These five vehicles were acquired in 1959 from the Hastings network owned by Maidstone & District Motor Services. They were standard Sunbeam products with electrical equipment by BTH and bodywork by Weymann. They were new to the south coast system in 1947/8. No. 85 was withdrawn in 1965 and no. 88 was taken out of service the following year. Upon purchase from Hastings, these vehicles had to have the power and brake pedals altered, as in Hastings the power pedal was on the right and the brake pedal on the left – this alteration brought them into line with the rest of the Maidstone vehicles.

When the first trolleybuses appeared on the streets of Maidstone they must have turned heads. The vehicles appeared so much bigger than the trams or indeed any of the contemporary petrol buses serving the county town. This is no.12 of the original Ransomes fleet before it left the works.

This scene presents an interesting comparison between the leading Ransomes vehicle and its English Electric stable mate at the rear. Note the differences in cab style and in the MAIDSTONE CORPORATION lettering. As is apparent, the two trolleybuses do have similar single mounts for both trolley poles.

This replica was produced as a promotional toy for a collectors' fair in the town. Although by no means contemporary with the prototype, this miniature gives a fair idea of the colours used in the late 1920s.

Corgi Collectables produced this 1:50 scale version of Maidstone trolleybus no.55 in its original state. As mentioned in the main text there have been a number of incarnations of the golden ochre/brown livery associated with the town.

This picture of no.56 lends itself for comparison with the model of no.55. The town coat of arms has been affixed to the side of the vehicle. As originally delivered in 1944, this particular trolleybus was furnished with wooden seating. More comfortable upholstered versions were installed shortly after the war. No.56 in rebodied state has since been preserved. *C. Carter*

No.68 is depicted in a livery style sometimes referred to as milk chocolate brown and white. Perhaps it was not the most attractive of the Maidstone colour schemes. This early 1950s view will be very familiar for those who remember being stuck in traffic jams, when the A20 cut through the middle of the town.

One of the ex Llanelli vehicles was numbered 83 in the Maidstone fleet; it lasted in service until late autumn 1960. According to some sources the corporation was ill advised in acquiring the two second hand purchases from South Wales. It was a surprise they survived as long as they did. *Peter Mitchell*

Ex Hastings nos.86 and 87 were withdrawn in the first two months of 1967. They were dumped outside the old tram shed on Loose Road. The entrances were boarded up, so that no human or inquisitive animal could investigate the interiors. No.86 was later rescued for preservation. *Peter Mitchell*

### Preserved Trolleybuses

The sad fate of demi-car tram 18 has already been noted, but several members of the trolleybus fleet were more fortunate and they escaped the attention of the scrappers. No.72 was preserved by the corporation and can now be seen at the National Trolleybus Museum, Sandtoft, near Doncaster. Former Brighton vehicle no.52 was saved by author and trolleybus enthusiast, Hugh Taylor. It now resides at the East Anglian Transport Museum at Carlton Colville, Suffolk. No.56 was rescued by A. Stevens and can be viewed at the National Trolleybus Museum.

Ex Brighton no.52 was also saved from extinction thanks to the efforts of Hugh Taylor. The elongated oval grill below the number plate suggested to some observers the mouth of a goldfish. Note the other form of electric traction in the shape of the Primrose & Len Dairy milk float. *Peter Mitchell*

## The Preservation of Trolleybus 52 by Hugh Taylor

The first time I saw Maidstone trolleybuses was on 14th October 1964; it was a rainy day so I didn't take many photos. My notebook states that one of the vehicles in service was number 52. At the time I was unaware of its provenance and did not know that it had been used in Brighton before coming to Maidstone. At the time I was a bus conductor with London Transport and found that it was worth visiting trolleybus systems in uniform as easy contact was made with drivers, conductors and maintenance staff – useful information was thus often gained. Brighton Corporation had used AEC trolleybuses (1-44) since inception in 1939. With new vehicles being required after the war they turned to BUT to supply them thereafter; in 1948, numbers 45 – 50 arrived. Nos.51 and 52 were delivered in chassis form in 1948, bodied in 1951 yet did not enter service until 25th March 1953.

In 1956, Brighton Corporation and Brighton Hove & District decided on a trolleybus replacement policy which occurred in two phases – one in 1959, the other in 1961. Both decided to withdraw their post-war vehicles before closure in order to command a good price on the second-hand market. Nos.51 and 52 were bought by Maidstone Corporation in February 1959 retaining the same fleet numbers with their new owners; this was the only instance of second-hand trolleybuses keeping the same numbers in their new homes. Having been repainted, 51 and 52 entered service later in the year. Many more visits to Maidstone ensued; my notebooks state that although I had taken many photos of 51, there were none of 52. On 1st August 1966, number 51 failed; it was parked up, withdrawn, in the old Loose tram shed. By now I had found out that 51 and 52 with their 120 horse power motors were so fast that they kept catching up other vehicles; consequently they spent much of the time in the depot. The problem was rectified by blanking off the top two of their thirteen notch contactors. It was not until 29th November 1966 that I had the opportunity to photograph and travel on 52.

I was intrigued by the fact that 52 had been delivered in chassis form in 1948 but did not enter service until 1953. Maidstone had not used it all that regularly due to its high horse power motor. Such an interesting vehicle needed to be saved; she was too good to be broken up. Transport undertakings can gain extra revenue by external advertising. What was 52 promoting latterly? 'Taylor made' whatever that was!

On 6th April 1967 number 52 was in service. I was using movie and still cameras to record trolleybus activities of the day. As the driver turned into the Bull Inn terminus at Barming he took it a bit too wide causing both poles to slip off the wires. This was on movie film – it was as if 52 was waving at me saying 'I know what you're hoping to do for me, thank you'.

Closure date was to be 15th April 1967. I made enquiries at Tonbridge Road depot as to how an approach should be made to obtain 52; I was advised to obtain a tender form which duly arrived in the post. Another Maidstone hairy (Doug Barrow) had obtained some classified information about how much some earlier vehicles had fetched – up to £120. It was going to be a stab in the dark as to what to tender so I offered £115. I sent a covering letter stating that the trolleybus would be for preservation rather than scrap hoping that would be taken into account by the Corporation. The tender had to be in to the Town Clerk of Maidstone by twelve noon on Friday 7th April 1967. A letter dated 12th April was sent to me stating that at the Transport Committee meeting of the previous night my tender was accepted – the letter was received on Thursday 13th April, with payment having to be made within four days. I made an appointment to see Walter Kershaw, the General Manager and Engineer on Friday 14th April, the penultimate day of operation. I paid £127 which was made up of a cheque for £100 and £27 in cash; the extra twelve pounds was for a set of six slave tyres. Mr Kershaw was very pleased to know 52 would not be scrapped and stated that both former Brighton trolleybuses had been good vehicles. I found out later that I'd tendered far higher than anybody else for any trolleybus that was for sale. The Transport Department must have been delighted that I'd offered so much. I wasn't bothered, as 52 was saved.

I asked Mr Kershaw if he would arrange for 52 to be in service on the last day. He said that all available vehicles would be working that day so that as many people as possible who wanted to travel on a trolleybus could do so. I arrived early on Saturday and yes – 52 was running. Now wasn't she on hire to the Corporation from me seeing I had paid for her the previous day! Unfortunately she broke down on the Parkwood Estate early in the morning and was towed back to the depot; it was disappointing as she was not due to run in until 11pm. Apparently she had suffered a few breakdowns in the previous few days but had been got going again (when I picked her up from the depot twelve days later the engineers had repaired her for me. They had traced the fault. Drivers were placing aluminium foil in the contactors; they had done this so as to lose a few journeys).

Brighton no.52 is depicted in 'as delivered' condition'

However, I did not have anywhere to house 52 – it was no good making arrangements if my offer failed. Terms of sale meant that vehicles had to be removed within twelve days of acceptance of the offer; little time was given between the time the tenders had to be in and when trolleybuses had to be removed. I was hoping to meet LTPS member Tony Belton on 15th April – very fortunately I met him at the depot gates in the evening. He was very pleased to know my news. I asked if there was anywhere it could go in the immediate future. There were some barns near Pluckley which was not all that far away – some LTPS vehicles were there and arrangements were soon made for 52 to join them. Tony had acquired a coach with the registration number KJH 900 which carried out all their tows; Tony drove it on all occasions.

The date set for the tow from Tonbridge Road depot was Thursday 27th April. By now the power had been switched off and members of staff pushed 52 onto Tonbridge Road while I was at the steering wheel. LTPS member Don Jones disconnected the prop shaft, KJH 900 hitched up to 52 and the journey to Pluckley commenced. As soon as we were out of sight of the depot a halt was made; the trolley arms were lifted onto the overhead and we travelled to the Fountain Inn at Barming in this mode. The booms were then lowered; 52 had been the last trolleybus to touch Maidstone overhead.

Number 51 and two other trolleybuses had been sold to a Mr M. Fairhurst of Bexhill-on-Sea for scrap and I contacted him on the basis of obtaining spare parts. He was very co-operative and said he would save breaking 51 till last; he arranged for it to be parked on the forecourt of Bexhill Railway Station. Another trip with KJH 900 saw LTPS members taking many units from 51 on 1st May. All seats and their frames were removed as were the 'Alhambrinal' ceiling panels, interior lamps, destination blinds, bamboo pole, handrails, strap hangers, contactor bank – even 51's headboard in the lower saloon. If we'd had the tools we'd probably have taken the booms as well. Mr Fairhurst did well out of the deal, for having taken many pounds off me he would also have got a good price for the rest of 51. Mr Fairhurst had also bid for my vehicle. Number 52 was taken to the East Anglia Transport Museum site at Carlton Colville in 1968 where she remains in service. It was a very well spent £127.

## Advertisements

It was common for British tramways to employ a skilled sign writer. Most operators derived valuable revenue by renting advertising spaces on their vehicles. The practice was widespread among municipal and company owned systems. It was once claimed that advertisements paid for the annual repaint of each tramcar. In the first months of the Maidstone tramways it was realised that several local businesses wished to advertise their wares on the new form of transport. On each dash either side of the fleet number the sign writer got to work. Early clients included the Lefevre Drapery Store in Stone Street and Walker's Furniture Emporium. At one stage Lefevre's dropped out making the cars look somewhat lop sided.

Advertising on the dashes ceased, when headlamps were moved to this location. From then on the upper deck decency boards sufficed for both hand painted and machine printed enamelled metal panels. Colours varied and to determine the hue of locally based firms' adverts is now well nigh impossible; however, national products such as BRASSO, BOVRIL, NUBOLIC SOAP and HUDSONS SOAP had country wide exposure and examples can be seen on the internet or in museum collections.

A well known Maidstone business was Thomas Grant and Sons of 31 Hart Street. The product names GRANTS MORELLO CHERRY BRANDY and GRANTS BOTTLED SPIRITS were displayed on the stair risers of some cars. As far as we can ascertain, the water car and the demi car never carried any advertising material.

A glance at the corporation's first motor buses reveals that they lacked advertisements. When double deck vehicles emerged on the scene the upper saloon side panels proved ideal for shops and businesses to advertise their wares. Over the years a gradual change was made to ready printed paper adverts; local brewers Fremlins took advantage of this situation. In the 1950s and 1960s inducements to purchase a number of well known products were pasted on buses and trolleybuses. These included DULUX PAINTS, WHITBREADS ALE & STOUT, LITTLEWOODS FOOTBALL POOLS, GOLDEN SHRED MARMALADE and various brands of cigarettes, which would not be permitted nowadays.

## Fares

Interviews with older Maidstonians in the 1970s and 1980s revealed many fond memories of the trams and their penny fares. This cheapness of travel for residents living to the west and south of the town centre was much appreciated.

Readers uncertain or unaware of pre decimal British currency in common use before 1971, should note that one pound was divided into twenty shillings. Each shilling was worth twelve pence. Below the value of the pound note there existed a number of coins. The lowest value coin in 1967 was the ha'penny (½d); there then followed the penny (1d), the thrupenny bit (3d), the sixpence (6d), the shilling (1s), the florin or two shilling piece (2s) and the half crown (2s 6d). The ten shilling (10s) note also existed, but anyone handing the conductor a ten shilling note for a simple bus or trolleybus fare would have been asked, sometimes quite forcibly, to tender something smaller! Colloquially, the use of the word 'quid' for pound and 'bob' for shilling was widespread. Hence the remark of a Maidstone bus inspector in 1966, that although the trolleybuses were going, they were still 'worth a few bob' as scrap value.

The original single fare to Barming was 2d and the return fare was 3d. As the tramway grew, a number of penny stages were introduced. On the Loose route a passenger could travel all the way for 2d, whilst there was a standard penny fare for any distance on the Tovil line. In July 1919 there was a small increase in fares on the Loose route, and this was followed in May 1920 by a general increase across all services. The through journey to Barming now cost 3d, while that to Tovil was raised by a halfpenny to 1½d. As mentioned in chapter three, there were from time to time special offers to encourage pleasure riding on the trams.

Fares remained stable after the introduction of the trolleybuses. A ticket from the town centre to Sutton Road cost 2d. Barming to Loose was 5d. Children under 14 travelled at half fare. There were concessions for working people and for students at the local schools. Further details of timetables and fares are displayed below.

## FARE TABLES
### LOOSE—PARK WOOD ESTATE—BARMING

```
Stage No.
 3  LOOSE
 4  2   Walnut Tree
 5  2 2   Papermakers
 6  3 2 2   Swan
 2  . . . . . .   Park Wood Estate
 3  . . . . . .  2   Bell Road
 4  . . . . . .  3 2   Nottingham Avenue
 5  . . . . . .  4 3 2   Grove Road
 6  . . . . . .  4 4 3 2   Cemetery Gates
 7  4 3 3 2 5 4 4 3 2   Wheatsheaf
 8  4 4 3 3 5 5 4 3 2 2   Plains Avenue
 9  5 4 4 4 6 5 5 4 3 3 2   Barton Road
10  5 5 4 4 6 6 5 5 4 3 3 2   Wrens Cross
11  6 5 5 5 7 6 6 5 4 4 4 3 2   High Street
12  6 6 5 5 7 6 6 5 4 4 3 3 2   West Station
13  6 6 6 5 7 6 6 6 5 5 4 3 3 2   Bower Street
14  6 6 6 6 8 7 6 6 6 5 5 4 4 3 2   Milton Street
15  7 7 6 6 8 7 7 6 6 6 5 4 4 3 2   Western Road
16  8 8 7 6 8 8 7 6 6 6 5 5 4 4 3 2   Fountain
17  8 8 8 7 9 8 8 7 7 6 6 5 5 4 3 2   Glebe Lane
18  8 8 8 8 9 9 8 7 7 6 6 6 5 5 4 3 2 BULL
```

The fares chart from 1961 shows that Maidstonians certainly had value for money in their public transport. The longest ride for an adult cost eight old pence (just over 3p)! Even before the end of the trolleybus era in 1967 fares had only risen by the odd halfpenny.

### TROLLEYBUS SERVICES
### MONDAY — FRIDAY  LOOSE—PARK WOOD—BARMING

[Timetable extract showing columns of pm departure times from Loose, Park Wood, Nottingham Avenue, Grove Road, Wheatsheaf, Cannon, West Station, Milton Street, Depot, Barming Fountain arr., and BARMING Bull arr., through afternoon and evening services. A note indicates "*—To Queens Monument."]

This extract from the 1961 official timetable shows the intensity of trolleybus services on a weekday afternoon and evening. Note the provision of rush hour short workings from Grove Road and Nottingham Avenue.

## Overhead Equipment

Unusually for Great Britain, Maidstone did not employ swivel head trolleys for its initial tramway from the town centre to Barming. The fixed head method demanded that the running wires were placed more or less centrally over the tram track. In practice this entailed the erection of span wires attached to traction standards positioned opposite one another. These traction standards had cast iron bases, which bore the town's coat of arms. On the Tovil and Loose routes the spun steel traction standards were plainer in design and lacked the cast iron bases. Distinctive fluted urn finials adorned the tops of the standards. Many of these finials survived through the trolleybus era and some can still be seen atop poles at the National Tramway Museum in Crich, Derbyshire.

The council's experience with fixed head trolleys may have influenced the decision to use conventional swivel heads on the second batch of tramcars ordered for the Tovil and Loose extensions. This allowed the overhead wiring to be moved off centre, because swivel heads permitted a fair degree of lateral movement, when following the overhead wire. Traditional bracket arm standards were employed on the new routes. The number of points or overhead frogs was limited, because double wires were hung over single track sections. This was quite usual British practice.

General Manager Lambert makes the following remarks concerning the conversion to trolleybuses:

The conversion of the whole of the overhead electrical equipment was carried out by the department, and although every span wire and fitting of the light railways has been replaced by new materials, no interference was caused to the tramway service.

The old steel poles have been reinforced with concrete, and on curves new poles have been supplied, of the medium and heavy types. Span wire construction throughout the route has been adopted. Most of the fittings are to MTA standards. The trolley wires are of 4/0 SWG grooved hard drawn cadmium copper, spaced 15 ins. apart and insulated from the span wires by the ordinary type of insulated bolt in the fittings and by porcelain between the wires and at the pole clips. The turning circles have been constructed to permit the vehicle to turn within a circle of 62ft. diameter at one of the termini and 68 ft. at the other. The original feeder for this route was only just capable of dealing with the load for the tramcars, so that it has been necessary to put in a new feeder, with ample capacity for dealing with a four minute service.

It was intended that the whole of the trolleybus system should be updated after the war by introducing the standard 24 inches spacing of the running wires and by the use of British Insulated Callender Cables steel spacer bars. However, this process was somewhat drawn out and took a number of years. Some overhead fittings were later purchased second hand from Brighton. Whereas the trams ran with a minimum of overhead frogs, the ones provided for trolleybuses were mostly manually operated. One of the characteristic acts of every trolleybus conductor was to descend from the back platform and hurry over to the pavement in order to pull the handle to change the overhead points. These handles were installed on traction standards just before intermediate turning circles or where the two routes bifurcated. Of course, this technology did not apply to trailing frogs. Electric points, controlled on the power or coast principle, were situated at the Wheatsheaf junction and at the Fountain turning circle, Barming.

Traction standards were usually thirty-one feet in length, although in some locations this height was exceeded. In Maidstone as in many other towns and cities they were mainly painted green, with the exception of those planted on the Bishops Way diversion and in the town centre, which were silver in colour. Span wires predominated, but there were bracket arms, principally on Gabriels Hill, Knightrider Street and Lower and Upper Stone Street. They were used extensively on the Parkwood loop,

Section feeds for the overhead were at roughly half mile intervals. Current was fed into the wires at 600 volts DC. There were sub stations at Tonbridge Road Depot, Fairmeadow, the Wheatsheaf junction and Sutton Road. Section boxes or circuit breaker boxes were installed on the pavement and could be opened by official key of one of the department's electrical staff. Inside each section box were isolating switches connected to the main traction supply. A peculiarity of Maidstone was the use of pillar section boxes dating from the tramway era.

Dismantling of the overhead was carried out by the council. Work continued throughout April and May 1967 and by 1st June the task was complete. Obviously, poles with street lamps were spared this destruction, otherwise unwanted standards were uprooted and carted away.

## Depots

It was a British linguistic convention, honoured by most operators, that trams and trolleybuses resided in depots, but motor buses were housed in garages. The Tonbridge Road tram depot originally consisted of a running shed with two tracks, which then terminated as a single line in an open yard at the back of the main building. In 1907 as a response to the expansion of the system, a further running shed with two extra tracks was added. When trolleybuses ousted the Barming trams, they were allotted space in the depot building directly opposite the entrance from Tonbridge Road. The remaining trams kept possession of the shed on the Queens Road side of the site.

When electric traction finally bowed out in 1967, the depot complex included a head office, a paint shop, a body shop, an electrical sub station, a cash office, a stores section and a crew room. In January 1969 the site was vacated and buses were moved to a new garage on Armstrong Road.

There was also a two road stabling shed for the trams on Loose Road. The building adjacent to Pickering Street certainly had a moribund appearance, according to George Gundry who passed that way in the summer of 1922. In the last few months of tramway operation the place was spruced up and resumed a more active role. In the 1960s out of service trolleybuses were stored here during the run down of the system.

Both former tram depots have now been demolished and housing occupies the sites.

Cars 1 and 2 are lined up at the depot prior to the inauguration of public service. This illustration is taken from a contemporary technical magazine. Looking past the trams there is a glimpse of the open yard behind the depot. The Tonbridge Road Depot was a simple functional building with the very minimum of ornamentation.

Pictured in the summer of 1983 the depot had not changed much; it took but little imagination to visualise the place still populated with tramcars. Tramlines are still in place and the troughs for trolleybus wires remain attached to the roof girders.

In the transition period from trams to trolleybuses the former tramway maintenance pits on the eastern side of the depot were planked over, so that no trolleybus wheels would accidentally sink into them. As we can see here, space was at a premium.

Since being demolished to give way to a residential development, a small section of tram track has been preserved. In 1983 there were more rails on view, such as the set of point blades illustrated here. A new generation of young local historians can measure the distance between the rails. When the tramway was constructed the gauge was set at three feet six inches, but most school kids nowadays would probably recognise the figure of 1067 millimetres.

The tram track layout can be clearly seen in this view of Loose Road Depot taken in 1963. After the trams ceased in 1930, it was not wired for trolleybuses.

All quiet at Tonbridge Road Depot, as trolleybus no.58 and a tower wagon rest in the sunshine. As can be seen there was not much room to manoeuvre in the yard. Note the original overhead wiring leading to the covered accommodation.

## The Southern Counties Touring Society

The Southern Counties Touring Society was formed by a number of transport enthusiasts and had a particular relationship with Maidstone. One of its presidents was Walter Kershaw, the Maidstone General Manager. John Meredith, himself a respected transport photographer and active member of the SCTS, reviews this society from its founding in 1947 to its dissolution some twenty years later:

William Crawforth was a Southern Railway train guard and was also a tram enthusiast. During the Second World War he took over the volunteer role of London Area Representative for the Light Railway Transport League, while the post holder was away on National Service. Will, as he was usually known, organised meetings and even some special tram tours, as wartime conditions would allow, notably at Southampton and Southend-on-Sea.

Once the war was over Will set up the Southern Counties Touring Society. The SCTS appealed to persons with an interest in local public transport systems that could be reached from London on day visits. As tramways were by then few in number, it was agreed to include bus and trolleybus operators as well. Right from the start in late 1947 visits were also arranged to industrial locations, not necessarily transport related. These included gas works, power stations, telephone exchanges, postal sorting offices, newspaper printing works and many more.

Will Crawforth acted as Secretary and Ernest Picton as Chairman. I was invited to assist with organising the special tours; the first one I organised was to Maidstone's small trolleybus system on Sunday 14th March 1948. At that time the last of their original fleet of three axle trolleybuses remained in the depot at Barming and members were incited to ride on and to photograph this vehicle. The SCTS went on to arrange further tours of Maidstone as their trolleybus operation was extended. These tours also included their motor buses. A particular favourite was their Crossley double deckers, a rare make in the south of England.

The SCTS had a number of tours of the much larger Hastings trolleybus network. A few elderly single deck vehicles were retained out of use at their Silverhill Depot in case they were needed again and members had the opportunity to go for a short ride and to photograph them. Hastings also retained an old open top trolleybus, but this vehicle was kept in a yard at Bulverhythe, well away from the overhead wires. However, we were able to stop nearby and at least we could climb aboard. Luckily the Hastings company realised the vehicle's potential and restored it.

The society prospered with tram tours of Birmingham, Cardiff, Grimsby & Immingham, Leicester, London, Sheffield and Southampton. Trolleybus tours ranged from Bournemouth to Doncaster, plus a dozen or more systems in between and countless tours by motor bus. The programme also included railway visits to motive power depots, signal boxes and other installations. Initially the railway tours were over minor lines such as Hellingly Hospital in East Sussex, Bowaters paper mill in Kent, and the Corringham Railway in Essex, but later progressed to full scale main line excursions.

Among the highlights was taking a Lord Nelson 4-6-0 on a rare visit to Exeter, a farewell tour over the Somerset & Dorset hauled by Evening Star, and introducing an Eastern Region A3 pacific locomotive to the south coast. A particular rarity was a steam hauled train over parts of the London Underground. This took place on a Sunday afternoon, 1st October 1961, and ran from Stanmore to New Cross Gate, including the section of the Inner Circle Line from Baker Street to Aldgate.

Many of the tours and visits were recorded on cine film and each year's films, entitled *Private Special* and the appropriate year, were first presented at the annual dinner, usually held at a prestigious location in central London.

The subsequent demise of the SCTS coincided with the growth of preservation activities with members taking a proactive role rather than the passive one of just seeing and photographing what public transport had to offer. However, in its heyday the society was held in high regard by local transport management and a number of general managers accepted the office of President, notably John Atherton of Eastbourne, Walter Kershaw of Maidstone and Wilfred Smith of Birmingham. Unfortunately, the cine film has been absorbed into a private collection, but still photographs of the SCTS's activities are frequently published.

The Maidstone tour of 14th March 1948 is commemorated in this photograph of SCTS and transport officials. A youthful John Meredith is standing on the extreme left of the group. *Jack Turley*

*Back cover* At Loose terminus in October 1966, the rear view of your author, then in his mid-teens, has been captured on film. I am operating my late father's wind up film camera, which had an embarrassing habit of stopping just at the vital moment. Luckily the clockwork mechanism stood up to the rigours of a trip to Maidstone and the resulting 8mm cine film remains as a lasting testament to a fine trolleybus system. *Richard Grover*

# Bibliography

**The Tramways of Kent Volume 1 – West Kent** by Invicta. Published in 1971 by the Light Railway Transport League & the Tramway and Light Railway Society.

**Maidstone and Chatham Tramways** by Robert J Harley. Published in 1994 by Middleton Press. ISBN 1873793405.

**The Maidstone Trolleybus** by D.J.S. Scotney. Published in 1972 by the National Trolleybus Association.

**The Trolleybuses of Maidstone** by Daniel Kain and Malcolm Coates. Published in 1972 by the British Trolleybus Society.

**75 Years of Municipal Transport in Maidstone** by Richard Lewis and Eric Baldock. Published in 1979 by the M&D and East Kent Bus Club.

**Maidstone Corporation Transport 1904-1974** by Eric Baldock. Published in 2012 by Amberley Publishing. ISBN 9781445608204.

**Maidstone Trolleybuses** by Robert J Harley. Published in 1997 by Middleton Press. ISBN 1901706001.

**Buses Illustrated December 1965.** Article entitled 'Maidstone in 300 Minutes' by F.W. York. Published by Ian Allan

**More Maidstone Memories** by R. Whitehead. Published in Old Motor November – December 1973.

**Maidstone Corporation and its Successors** – An illustrated history 1904-1992 by N. King. Published in 2004 by the M&D and East Kent Bus Club.

**Lost Tramways of Kent** by L. Opitz. Published in 2004 by Countryside Books.

**Tramcar Liveries** by G.E. Baddeley. Published in 1977 by the Tramway and Light Railway Society.

**Trackless to Trolleybus** by Stephen Lockwood. Published in 2011 by Adam Gordon. ISBN 9781874422860.

**Works Tramcars of the British Isles** by David Voice. Published in 2008 by Adam Gordon. ISBN 9781874422716

All students of public transport in Maidstone owe a great debt to D.J.S. Scotney, whose meticulous research was published in *The Tramways of Kent* and *The Maidstone Trolleybus*.

Although some of the books listed are out of print, many can still be obtained through the internet at abebooks.com or on the second hand market. Moving images of the vehicles at work are available in the Online Video entitled *No Trolleys to Loose*.

A very useful resource for plans of British tramcars, plus other scale modelling items is Terry Russell – www.terryrusselltrams.co.uk

The following guide books also contain useful information about local public transport:

**Maidstone Official Guide** by L.R.A. Grove and Alfred Joyce. First Edition published by G.W. May Ltd.

**Maidstone – The Homeland Handbooks.** Published in 1912 by Frederick Warne.

**A Guide to the Borough of Maidstone** by A.S. Lamprey. Published in 1914 by Walter Ruck.